Film Is Content
A Study Guide for the Advanced ESL Classroom

Julia A. Williamson
Jill C. Vincent

Ann Arbor
THE UNIVERSITY OF MICHIGAN PRESS

Copyright © by the University of Michigan 1996
All rights reserved
ISBN 0-472-08330-9
Library of Congress Catalog Card No. 95-61871
Published in the United States of America by
The University of Michigan Press
Manufactured in the United States of America

1999 1998 1997 1996   4 3 2 1

No part of this publication may be reproduced, stored
in a retrieval system, or transmitted in any form or by
any means, electronic, mechanical, or otherwise
without the written permission of the publisher.

Illustrations by Holly Jean

We dedicate this book to our families, especially to the memory of George Tate Williamson.

Preface

Film Is Content: A Study Guide for the Advanced ESL Classroom is meant to serve as a beginner's guide to film interpretation and discussion for high intermediate and advanced students. It is arranged by genre and by theme into units of four films each. This text thus lends itself especially well to the content or elective class that meets three to five hours per week. (By *content* we mean those classes devoted to realia in a whole language approach, as opposed or in addition to the traditional methods of teaching the individual skill areas of grammar, reading, listening/speaking, and writing.) It could also be used as a resource for teachers who have limited preparation and screening time but who wish to use film as an additional activity in so-called regular classes. Additionally, students who wish to view films on their own outside of the classroom will also be interested in having this text in their personal libraries.

For years, language teachers have relied upon audiovisuals to further their students' mastery of the target language, and there is a growing market of audiocassettes, videos, and interactive video games from which to choose. These inherently helpful technologies should be used to greatest advantage. Movies, especially, should be exploited because of their built-in entertainment value and wide availability. The purpose of this book, then, is to provide teacher and student a way to use the video medium. To that end we have chosen for inclusion here films that are readily available in video stores. Uncut, unsimplified, and shown in their entirety they provide authentic texts for critical study. Before you show a film to your class, you should check with your media center to find out if there is an established policy at your school for showing films. While policies may vary from institution to institution, it seems reasonably clear among copyright specialists that there is a distinction made between "public" use and "classroom" use of films. Classroom use means instructional/educational use. In other words, the film is not being shown for entertainment purposes or for cultural improvement, only for educational purposes. Of course, it goes without saying, copies cannot be made and distributed to the students. Remember, first check with your school's media center or your department to verify there is no policy against using films in your classroom for educational purposes.

Our text is unique because it offers a wide variety of many films, yet at the same time demonstrates the interconnectedness of these works. This approach is in keeping with schema theory that, in brief, holds that the learner builds upon existing background knowledge. The method of introducing multiple films on the same topic demonstrates to the student that films are sometimes formulaic, that they are made for the critical viewing pleasure of the audience, and that they are to be analyzed for content as well as to be viewed for amusement. The genre approach allows students to search for recurrent features in plot, character, setting, theme, directorial style, and so on. Additionally, it allows the students to see how a genre has developed and changed with the passage of time. In this text, the films of each genre/chapter are arranged chronologically, from the oldest to the most recent, for this very purpose.

Another distinguishing quality of this book is that it employs the whole language approach to learning. Historically, ESL teachers have used film in the classroom for very skills-specific reasons, for instance, showing a small portion of the film as a point of departure for listening comprehension, or for considering facets of American culture, informal language, or discrete grammar points in a particular dialogue. Rarely have ESL students been challenged to actually analyze a film, either in its totality, or in more substantial chunks.

We acknowledge, with gratitude, the support of our colleagues at Maryville College and the University of Tennessee, with special thanks to Ilona Leki, Robert Hutchens, and Kelly Franklin. Last, but certainly not least, we thank the students of MCCELL, who inspired this project.

Contents

1. **Introduction: A Teacher's Guide** 1
   How to Use the Materials in This Text 1
   Postviewing Activities 5
   Approaches to Film Criticism 6
   Film Terminology 8
2. **Classic Films** 10
   King Kong (1933) 13
   Laura (1944) 21
   High Noon (1952) 27
   Some Like It Hot (1959) 35
3. **Feminism and the Feminist Film** 40
   Pat and Mike (1952) 45
   9 to 5 (1980) 49
   Working Girl (1988) 55
   Thelma and Louise (1991) 59
4. **Discrimination in Film** 64
   Freaks (1932) 69
   Forbidden (1985) 75
   The Accused (1988) 79
   Do The Right Thing (1989) 85
5. **Aspects of the Romantic Comedy** 91
   Bachelor Mother (1939) 95
   The Thrill of It All (1963) 99
   What's Up, Doc? (1972) 103
   Moonstruck (1987) 107
6. **Hitchcock Films: The Auteur Genre** 111
   Notorious (1946) 115
   Rear Window (1954) 121
   North by Northwest (1959) 125
   Psycho (1960) 129
7. **Suspense Films** 135
   Charade (1963) 137
   D.O.A. (1988) 143
   Traces of Red (1992) 149
   Cape Fear (1991) 155

Additional Film Units for Consideration 161
Appendix 164
References 165
Quizzes 167

Chapter 1
Introduction: A Teacher's Guide

How to Use the Materials in This Text

Thoroughly presenting a film, that is, viewing it, discussing it, and analyzing it takes several classroom hours. A typical content class meeting four to five hours a week would, ideally, cover one film per week. To stay within this time frame, teachers may wish to follow the teaching strategy mapped out here.

1. Have a previewing discussion that can be approached in the same fashion as prereading. A topic or theme of the movie can be presented and discussed by the group. Any vocabulary pertinent to the subject should, as it arises, be noted on the board. For instance, *King Kong*, as a representation of the horror film genre, could begin with a discussion of horror films in general, with particular stress on the characteristics of such films. The subject of animal rights and animal cruelty would also be relevant.

2. Before handing out any of the text material on the film, write the title on the board. Ask students to predict the film's content from the title. Often a title will be culturally obscure, will contain a lexical item unfamiliar to the students, or will be an example of double entendre. The film title *What's Up, Doc?* is, to a native English speaker and cartoon connoisseur, immediately recognizable as a quote from Bugs Bunny, but it's not clear what Bugs says in translation. The meaning of the title of Hitchcock's *Notorious* is another mystery to students and should be explained both literally and figuratively. A further example is the acronym D.O.A., which serves as the ironic title of the film.

3. Referring to this text, have students focus on the characters' names, along with some basic background information about their personality traits and relationships with each other. In *Moonstruck*, for instance, it is

important that the students know about the bad blood between Ronny and Johnny Cammareri and that they have some knowledge of Loretta's past, because the plot and comic relief hinge on the interactions of those three characters.

4. After introducing the characters, review with the students the basic plot line. Some plots, like those in a suspense film, are long and complex and should be reviewed, prior to the screening, in sections rather than in their entirety. However, every film needs at least a thumbnail plot sketch, with particular emphasis on the opening scenes. Such pertinent information includes the time and setting. If the time frame or era is important to the story, it should be explained in advance. *High Noon*, for example, is a western period piece, but it also employs actual or real time, adding to the drama and suspense. Setting can be crucial too, as is the case with *Psycho* and the Gothic house on the hill overlooking the unimposing Bates Motel.

5. The four previous previewing steps may take up as much as an hour's time. At this point, though, the students should be ready to begin viewing the film. Keep in mind the "Notes" section for each film and interject that information as it becomes relevant. Some of the notes are best reserved until film's end as part of the postviewing discussion, but occasionally an interruption is necessary. For example, in viewing movies of a certain genre, the teacher should probably pause at those points in the narrative that clearly display any characteristic unique to that genre. To illustrate, in the romantic comedies the teacher's emphasizing the visual humor, explaining the witty rejoinders of the main characters, and pointing out the mocking or cynical tone in their voices is important in establishing in the students' minds some of the features of that genre.

6. A film's being well received by the students is largely a function of the teacher's knowing when to hit the pause button. Too many interruptions are distracting. Students are not going to understand every line of dialogue, every idiomatic expression, or every cultural reference. It isn't necessary that they come away from the film too thoroughly immersed in its subtleties, since their doing so would be time consuming and would cause distraction from the main goal of acquiring the basic tools for film analysis. Some lines of dialogue are, on the other hand, crucial to the plot and should be reviewed and explained. This is a judgment call. Some recurrent vocabulary items or slang expressions may also be necessary to a complete understanding of a particular character. Certain references to culture or certain behaviors unfamiliar to the students should be explained. Hitting pause can become an art form. Learning to read the expressions of confusion and to distinguish blank stares on the students' faces is immensely helpful in determining when to pause and explain. Encourage students to ask for clarification.

There are other causes for pause. Taking time out to call attention to camera angles and shots, explained in more detail later in this introduction, is occasionally advisable. Camera work is particularly important in Hitchcock. For instance, any time Hitchcock goes for a high-angle shot, the audience knows something conspiratorial or illegal is afoot, as in *Psycho* when Marion retires to the ladies' room of the used car lot to unobtrusively extract a few bills from the wad she has stolen from her boss. And close-ups are just as significant. In Hitchcock's *Notorious* the camera often focuses in close-up on teacups, beverage glasses, and wine bottles because drinking in its many forms is a plot device that helps move the action forward. It is also well worth the pause to point out to students Hitchcock's cameo appearances, which are meant to draw attention to some important aspect of the film. In *North by Northwest*, for example, the audience sees Hitchcock getting on a bus. This emphasizes and foreshadows the amount of traveling in store for the main character.

It is also a good idea to do a plot check periodically to determine the students' overall comprehension of the story line and to remind them of any significant details they may not have yet grasped. For suspense films this is immensely important.

7. Before viewing the film, and during the course of the screening, it would be wise to introduce a few key vocabulary items. Because the purpose of this text is to teach students to analyze film, not to increase their word power, emphasis on students' acquiring a substantial number of new lexical items should be downplayed. However, certain words and phrases are often crucial to their understanding. For instance, *Pat and Mike* is a film about the world of sports, especially golf, tennis, and boxing; thus a list of pertinent sporting terms ought to be included. It also includes a lot of nonessential and outdated but nonetheless very amusing slang like "to get frazzled," "to race your motor," "to get a word in edgewise," and so on. Other films are also fraught with idiomatic expressions that sometimes deserve interpretation. Among them are *Some Like It Hot*, *Thelma and Louise*, *Do The Right Thing*, and *Bachelor Mother*. Still other films contain lexical items that help define the characters in some way. For example, in *9 to 5* the male lead, Frank Hart, is continually described as a "sexist, egotistical, lying, hypocritical bigot." To understand his character students should be aware of the meaning of those words. Sometimes vocabulary items help carry forward the plot. To illustrate, in *Notorious* it is necessary that the students know the meaning of the terms *metallurgist*, *metal ore*, *traitor*, *treason*, and *betray* in order to follow the motivations of the Nazi spies. In more recent movies there is also the additional lexical dimension of obscenity, which must be approached with

some discretion. The films of this text that contain a generous smattering of the street vernacular include *Thelma and Louise*, *The Accused*, *Do The Right Thing*, *Cape Fear*, and *Traces of Red*.

8. With every film it is important to keep in mind the six elements of fiction since film and literature can be analyzed in much the same fashion. Consider:

a) *Plot.* The story line, consisting of the exposition (introduction of the characters and setting), the rising action (the point at which the conflict is introduced), the climax, the falling action (the conflict is resolved), and the conclusion. Of course this pattern varies from film to film, and the variations themselves are worthy of discussion. The suspense film relies heavily on plot development, for example.

b) *Characters.* The actors, who may be of two types: *round*, well-developed, three-dimensional, or *flat*, about whom almost nothing is known. Generally there is at least one *protagonist*, the hero or heroine, and one or more *antagonists*, opponents or adversaries of the leading character. It is important to note that movies contain, by necessity, both round and flat characters, but that the more allegorical types of films, such as westerns, contain very few well-developed characters.

c) *Setting.* The place and time of the action. In some movies setting is almost irrelevant; in others, Hitchcock's *Psycho* among them, the setting is crucial.

d) *Point of view.* The narrator (if any) of the story. Most movies have no narrator, although it is clear that the audience is being manipulated to feel sympathy for and identify with certain of the main characters. *Film noir* pictures frequently have a narrator, as do more recent films of the suspense genre, such as *Traces of Red*.

e) *Style.* This can include many elements: music, motifs (musical, verbal, or visual), mood, symbolism, foreshadowing, as well as the very broad category of directorial style.

f) *Theme.* The main idea. Because the theme is so integral to the total comprehension of a film, and because the theme and subthemes are often difficult for students to articulate, the major themes of each film in this text are delineated for them.

9. After viewing the film, use the quiz as a springboard for in-class discussion or as a take-home exam. The quiz requires some time and thought to answer, but the guides in the text provide most of the information needed to complete the tests properly.

Postviewing Activities

Try some of the following strategies after screening the film. The activities listed here are meant to serve as a more extensive unit of study involving reading or listening and speaking.

1. *Role-play.* Have the students assume the roles of various characters in the film and act out a scene. Or have them create a character role for themselves and enact any real-life situation, so long as they stay "in character."
2. *Make a Hollywood Minute.* In a form of role play, have one student act as a Rona Barrett type and interview another student who is either acting as a character from the film or pretending to be the actor who is portraying the character in the film.
3. *Retell the story.* Have the students attempt to retell the story. Students work in groups and note the main events chronologically. Then the two (or more) groups present their lists while the teacher writes everything in sequence on the board. Encourage groups to interrupt in order to add information, or to correct or clarify details.
4. *Change the ending.* Help students come up with alternative endings. This may be facilitated by changing the focus. Have them pretend the story revolved around another character other than the protagonist and ask how the change in point of view would have affected the ending. Hitchcock films will work here: have the students imagine that the "bad guys" accomplish their foul purpose.
5. *Keep a film journal.* For each film the students watch, have them informally record their impressions, which may include the good and bad points, exciting scenes, scintillating characters, new vocabulary words, and so on.
6. *Argue/debate.* Divide the class into two or more groups to prepare to argue some controversial issue. A talk-show format could also be created as a means of debating the issue. Films in the unit on discrimination are especially suited to this arrangement.
7. *Discuss cultural and universal values.* Have a discussion of any significant American cultural values particularly evident in the film; i.e., identify values common to the target culture. *Bachelor Mother*, for instance, exemplifies values of the 1930s and *Cape Fear*, family values of the 1980s and 1990s.
8. *Read film reviews.* Teach students how to use the *Reader's Guide to Periodical Literature* or one of the other sources of movie news and reviews listed in the appendix so that they can locate and read film reviews. Ask them to assess the film reviewer's basic impression of

the movie and then agree or disagree with it. It would be best if they could find two reviews of each film and perhaps make note of the differences in style and opinion. Have them further note the style of the critiques and what is praised and criticized. Ask what they, as film critics, would have mentioned in the review.

9. *Write an essay.* For writing practice, suggest an essay comparing two or more films or characters. The unit on feminism works well in this regard.
10. *Research the historical time frame*. To get a better idea of the film setting, have students scout around the library for information on the period. *High Noon* is set in the Old West. *Pat and Mike* takes place in the 1950s and focuses on the popularity of professional sports at that time. *Notorious* takes a look at Nazi spy activities in Brazil just after World War Two.
11. *Survey the populace.* Have students create a questionnaire to use on the campus population. The questions would be simple and would concern whether or not the interviewee had seen the film, what was thought of it, and whether or not it should be recommended to the general public. A rating scale could be included.
12. *Create a flick.* Have the students write a synopsis of a movie they would like to make. The dialogue and staging directions for one or two scenes would be enough.

Approaches to Film Criticism

These approaches are included for use with the more advanced students to provide a springboard for other writing assignments or academic discussions.

The first approach, called the Journalistic Approach, is more a review than a critique. As its name implies, it is the method employed by the media. The treatment is topical and includes such information as the director, producer, writer, and actors and their roles. Assessment of the film rests largely upon whether the reviewer likes it or not and for what reasons. Any review from a mainstream magazine or newspaper will easily illustrate this approach (Bywater and Sobchack 1989, 3–4).

Another critique style, the Humanist Approach, discusses the film in more depth, including an interpretation of theme, symbols, etc. In this case aesthetics are to be considered over mass appeal. Humanists look for the "emotional and intellectual experience of the film" in order to find human values and universal truths such as love, loss, joy, grief, death. It is a broad, general sort of critique (Bywater and Sobchack 1989, 24–27).

A third form of criticism is the <u>Auteur Approach,</u> which describes and evaluates the director's work in terms of technique, style, and film content. Most criticism of this kind follows the historical pattern of the director's body of work, noting the consistencies, the recurrences, and the evolution of that director's films over his/her lifetime. When taking this approach one should look for the amount of material about the auteur and consider the themes employed, the stars and crew worked with, the filmmaking techniques used, and any personal touches (Bywater and Sobchack 1989, 51–54).

A fourth category, the <u>Genre Approach,</u> describes and classifies film forms and types, grouping films by story lines, characters, settings, or themes. Genre criticism generally attempts to find, categorize, and explain the characteristics and history of the genre as it has evolved. For that reason most chapters of this text include at least one older film, to establish historic perspective. To study a genre is to look for certain specific recurring features of plot, character, setting, theme, and dialogue, and to note any actors who fit definitely into the genre, to be aware of any sociological undertones, and to observe how the genre has developed or changed over the years (Bywater and Sobchack 1989, 80–82).

A fifth and more scholarly approach, the <u>Social Science Approach</u>, defines the film's psychology. It explains how the film mirrors the society and attempts to find the more profound reasons, be they sociological, psychological, or mythical, for its popularity. This approach also takes into consideration the importance of moviegoing to the social life of the people and tries to figure in the influence video rentals and cable TV have had on the film. Another important consideration is how women and minorities are dealt with in the film, i.e., whether they are stereotyped or treated within a realistic framework (Bywater and Sobchack 1989, 109–15).

A sixth, the <u>Historical Approach</u>, handles the description and analysis of film since its inception, the changes over time, and the historical impact of film. Film is artifact in this approach. This form of critique asks how the various aesthetic aspects come together to become a movement, how genres start and how they change as time passes, how film influenced certain historic time frames, like the Great Depression, and whether those films merely reflected the times or influenced them (Bywater and Sobchack 1989, 138–41).

A final form of film criticism, the <u>Ideological/Theoretical Approach</u>, ponders the film medium's relationship to culture. It encompasses film theory. Focus might be on feminist, Marxist, or neo-Freudian theory. This approach is film as film, and film as a sociopolitical or ideological vehicle.

This sort of criticism considers the relation of the viewer to the film, the effect of the film on a deep psychological level, the representation of women realistically, the idealization or lack thereof of the real world, the bipolar opposites represented, such as light and dark, good and evil, male and female (Bywater and Sobchack 1989, 162–65).

This text uses a combination of all those approaches in an attempt to give students and teachers a well-rounded guide to understanding and interpreting the movies, and thus the world, around them.

Film Terminology

We include this section for purposes of providing the truly advanced students with a means of acquiring a more thorough understanding of the film and its direction. André Bazin, French critic, once remarked that "one way of understanding better what a film is trying to say is to know how it is saying it" (Giannetti 1982, 6). Form includes the camera work or cinematography [shots, angles, lighting, or color].

Shots

Extreme long shot. Sometimes called an "establishing shot," as it shows the setting.

Long shot. The same distance, for instance, as between the audience and the stage. Directors (like Hitchcock) who like to arrange people and objects inside a limited space use this often.

Medium shot. Shows only the upper body of the actor. It is useful for making expository [introductory] scenes.

Close-up. Focuses on only one object—no background. It is used to stress the significance of an object or person, sometimes making the object look bigger or more important.

Extreme close-up. Focuses very closely on the object or person, for added emphasis.

Deep-focus shot/wide-angle shot. Everything seen at a short, medium, and far distance at the same time, and all clearly in focus. This way the director is guiding the viewer's eye from one object to another, but with all objects equally focused. No judgment is being made by the camera.

Angles

Bird's-eye view. A scene photographed from up above. The viewer is like God, looking down from a morally superior setting.

High-angle. Overhead, but not as high. The setting seems more important and the people below seem less significant.

Low-angle. The opposite of high-angle. Objects appear taller. Violent scenes can look more confusing. Persons photographed at this angle command fear or respect.

Eye-level shot. No angles. Angles imply judgments, so in this sort of shot the audience forms their own opinions.

Oblique angle. Camera is tilted so that a person or thing appears to be about to fall over. This angle is used for point-of-view shots and suggests tension, instability, movement, and anxiety (Giannetti 1982, 8–16).

Other Technical Terms of Interest

Dissolve. A new scene gradually replaces another one, so that at one point both scenes appear to be blended together.

Dolly or tracking shot. The camera moves forward and/or backward.

Fade-in. The whole scene of a film becomes gradually visible as the screen gets lighter.

Fade-out. The opposite.

Flashback. A scene or scenes included in the film that take the audience back in time before the present action/time.

Flash-forward. A scene that takes the audience forward in time to a future scene in the movie.

Freeze frame. Action stops and instead of a moving picture there is a photo. The director's aim is to focus attention on a particular image.

Panning. The camera moves across a scene slowly from left to right or right to left, up to down or down to up.

Reaction shot. As one character is speaking, or as an action is happening, the camera turns to show us the reaction of the character who is affected by the speech or action.

Slow motion. The action of the scene is slowed down for emphasis. Usually slow motion denotes tragedy.

Subjective shot. The camera is the character. We see what he or she sees and thus identify strongly (Bywater and Sobchack 1989, 222–34).

Chapter 2
Classic Films

The Horror Film Genre

Between the 1930s and the 1980s the horror film was slowly transformed [changed]; i.e., it passed through certain phases as a genre. To define this film category, therefore, all stages of its development must be understood. First, however, the story, or narrative, itself, which has not changed during all those years, must be explained. It has a three-part format. Initially [first], some sort of lack of stability appears in a "normal" environment. Next, the main characters fight to get back their formerly secure position. Finally, stability is returned and the danger is destroyed. This third part has actually often been ignored in cinema of recent times. Often it isn't clear at film's end what will ultimately happen to the protagonists (Tudor 1991, 17–18).

The first phase of the horror movie was 1931–36. In this stage the threat [danger] to stability was *outside* the audience. It was usually far away in some European setting, such as Transylvania. Usually the films of this period were "mad [insane]-scientist movies," such as Frankenstein monster movies. This type of film was composed of several key factors: (*a*) the scientist, working night and day, looking for the secrets to creating life; (*b*) a monster, created accidentally; (*c*) a handicapped aid to the scientist who stirs the anger of the monster; (*d*) two youthful protagonists (usually male and female) who have only a small role; (*e*) an experimental lab that is usually isolated from the town and has lots of scientific equipment; and (*f*) local inhabitants who protest the creature's existence and work together to try to destroy it (Tudor 1991, 28–29).

This classic film period was followed by the war period, 1941–46, when films were made quickly rather than carefully and on a low budget. Many of the earlier classic films were borrowed from but the resulting plots became ridiculous. During this time of formulaic [made by pattern, using a formula] pieces, vampire films such as *Dracula* lost popularity and the preferred bad guy was either a scientist playing around with nature or a supernatural figure [ghost], the emphasis being the idea of life after death (Tudor 1991, 33–34, 37).

The next phase of the horror film began about 1956 and lasted until 1960. The threat to stability came from outer space this time. (Possibly this was a response to Americans' real fear of a communist invasion or atomic blast.) Mad-scientist/monster films became popular again but with one major difference: the scientists were more sympathetically presented and science was seen as a learning tool rather than as something to fear (Tudor 1991, 39, 42).

The fourth phase (1963–66) focused on insanity. In many of these films what appears to be a ghost is, in actuality, a mad person hidden away from society, perhaps in a big, Gothic house. Mad-scientist movies also continued, and science was found to be irresponsible, creating giant monsters as a result of atomic testing. The Godzilla creature is a good example. He even meets King Kong in 1963 in *King Kong versus Godzilla* (Tudor 1991, 49–53).

The next stage is marked by the years 1971–74 and in many ways is just a continuation and intensification of the supernatural, or of the theme of madness. However, the insanity, or psychosis, is treated differently in this phase. Attempts are made to understand and explain the madness rather than to immediately label [name] the affected character as evil. Typical of this phase of horror movies is excess: more bloody violence and more sex. One interesting new twist in the genre is the threat of nature getting out of control not because of atomic testing and radiation, but because of the various types of pollution humans have dumped into their environment (Tudor 1991, 56–62).

In the last phase, psycho movies continue to dominate, particularly due to the influence of *Halloween* in 1979 and the series of *Friday the 13th* movies beginning in 1980. There are still a few films that deal with scientific research gone crazy, hazardous waste dumping, and the creatures created from experiments with toxic substances (Tudor 1991, 68, 72).

King Kong was a kind of "prehistoric monster subgenre" (Tudor 1991, 37). It appears that this subgenre has recently made a very explosive comeback [return] with the film *Jurassic Park* (1993). In any case, the narrative aspects are the same. The monster is an external threat that invades and menaces the established social order, causing chaos. However, monsters do often elicit the audience's sympathies, for they do not intentionally [purposefully] try to wreak havoc [cause damage] but instead are provoked and therefore retaliate [fight back] as any threatened animal would (118).

Previewing Questions
King Kong

1. How does the narrative [story] follow the three-part format mentioned in the explanation of the horror film genre at the beginning of this chapter?
2. Consider the proverb in the film's opening scene. How is it significant to the theme?
3. In what ways might Kong be symbolic?

King Kong

(1933) dirs. Merian Cooper, Ernest Schoedsack   100 min.
Starring: Fay Wray, Bruce Cabot

Setting: New York City and Skull Island, during the Great Depression (1929–40).

Characters

Carl Denham [Robert Armstrong]—a fearless filmmaker who has traveled the world to make authentic motion pictures. Not only is he brave but he is also ruthless [without morals]. He will do anything to make a movie that the public likes. For instance, (*a*) he hires Ann because the critics said he could make more money by having romance and a love interest in his next picture; and (*b*) he smuggles [illegally transports] lots of dynamite onto the boat, even though doing so is prohibited.

Ann Darrow [Fay Wray]—an unemployed actress. Ann, like many people of the Depression era, has no food or money. Carl exploits [uses] her neediness by hiring her to go on a long, dangerous voyage [trip]. She's an orphan [parentless], so no one will miss her if she disappears.

Jack Driscoll [Bruce Cabot]—one of the young sailors on the ship that Denham rents to take him and his crew to Skull Island.

Plot

In search of a mythical [unreal, fairy-tale] creature he has heard about, Carl Denham leaves with his new "star," Ann Darrow, and his film crew for a place called Skull Island. It's an uncharted [unmapped] island somewhere west of Sumatra named for a mountain there that is skull shaped. There is rumored to be a great wall built by the natives to keep out a monster they call "Kong." Denham doesn't tell his crew anything about this until they've been out at sea for six weeks.

They arrive at the island just at the time the natives are preparing to make a tribal offering to Kong, their god. When they see the golden-haired Ann, they believe she will be a better offering than the dark-skinned young woman whom they have already chosen for Kong. When Denham refuses to give Ann to the natives, they come in the night to the ship and kidnap her and offer her to Kong.

Denham and his men try to rescue her, but they have to fight too many monsters, including Kong. All the men in the rescue party are killed except Denham and Driscoll. Driscoll gets the idea to capture Kong and take him back to civilization for exhibition. He promises the men that they will all become millionaires.

Back in New York, Ann and Kong become instantly famous as "Beauty and the Beast." But the popping and flashing of the photographers' bulbs make Kong think they're trying to hurt Ann, who is his love object, so he breaks through his chains and runs destructively through the city of New York, searching for and attempting to protect his woman.

Notes

- Like many of the early horror films, *King Kong* opens with a proverb [wise teaching]: "And the beast looked upon the face of beauty, and lo, his hand was stayed from killing. And from that day forward, he was as one dead" (Zinman 1970, 172). The idea of this Arabian proverb is that beauty and love have a civilizing influence, by killing all violent and wild intentions.

- Notice how the music works to build our excitement.

- There are many instances of foreshadowing [a technique whereby the audience is shown something that will later be very significant]. For example: (*a*) Ann's "practice" scream on the boat and later her real screams; (*b*) the fateful statement "Suppose it [Kong] doesn't like having its picture taken . . ." that later proves true; (*c*) the proverb at the film's beginning; and (*d*) Iggy the pet monkey on the boat, who foreshadows the main attraction.

- The city in this film is portrayed as corrupt and the cause of alienation.

- King Kong was a product of 1930s technology. Very small models of Kong were used to simulate the giant ape. These models, made of rubber and sponge, had movable parts, even animated facial features. The huge Kong of the movie was really an eighteen-inch miniature. After each movement, the model was photographed, the camera was stopped, and the model was reset. Thus the animal appeared to be moving, but it took hours and hours of shooting just to show Kong taking a few steps. For the scenes in which an actor had a close-up with the beast, a giant statue and hand of Kong were used (Zinman 1970, 171, 173).

- In the final scenes, as Kong fights the airplanes off (i.e., as civilization is destroying him) he isn't the oppressor anymore. Instead he is the victim. He is alone, defeated by modern civilization and frustrated by lost love. Kong was big and brave and loyal and pure in his love for Ann. Kong is a tragic figure. Back home on his island he was a god, a primitive innocent fighting for survival. Kong was lord of all his territory. He was noble and good. Although exploited, he never became immoral or unclean like Denham (Zinman 1970, 173).

- None of the characters is very well developed. They are all flat and basically representative of a type rather than of a specific, individualized human being. These types are as follows:

   Ann—the woman/sex object
   Jack—the common man with a good heart
   Carl—the corrupting influence of society

   Therefore, this film is, in one way, an allegory [a story in which the message is more important than the characters]. The many themes in this film suggest that the directors were more interested in our interpretation, in our receiving the messages, than in our identifying with the characters.

- Interestingly, Miss Fay Wray (Ann Darrow) felt that King Kong should have been classified as an adventure fantasy rather than as a horror film. She said, "If Kong were purely a horrifying and horrible fellow, the sympathy he evokes when, finally, he is struck down wouldn't exist. There is no doubt about such sympathy" (Zinman 1970, 172).

- Most quotable quote: As Kong lies dead, a policeman notes that "The airplanes got him [Kong]." Denham retorts, "It was Beauty killed the Beast" (Zinman 1970, 174).

- *King Kong* is one of the most widely known and oft-seen movies in history. It was remade in 1976, and other, earlier, versions used and abused the image of King Kong in such "B" [second-rate] movies as *Son of Kong* and *King Kong meets Godzilla*.

Themes

- Interpretations:

   —From a psychological point of view, the Empire State Building is a giant phallic [phallus=penis] symbol and represents the id [the uncivilized side of human nature]. If this interpretation is correct, Kong could be the id, the representation of the beast inside each human being. We humans go through life smoothly. Then we fall in love, which is accompanied by sex, which is bestial and uncivilized, the product of our id. Note, for instance, that the beast doesn't appear on screen until Jack has found love. Love brings out the beast in him and he must conquer it. As he rescues Ann, he is saving her from the beast inside himself. They escape by jumping into the water, which is a symbolic cleansing [washing]. Such an examination of humans', especially males', inner nature was very common among early horror films and served to emphasize the fight within each of us between good and evil.

—From a sociological point of view, Kong can be seen as symbolic of the natural human being. The message, then, is that society is ruining [destroying] our natural, innocent selves, making us powerless and sexless. Others interpret Kong as representing the poor and oppressed [exploited] workers of the Great Depression. Still others say the film has racial overtones and that Kong represents black people, because, like them, he is captured by white men and exploited in their white world (Zinman 1970, 172).

—From a feminist point of view, woman is always an object, which reflects a chauvinistic [male dominant] perspective. Ann spends much of her screen time screaming helplessly. She is a victim, exploited by Denham and lusted after by Jack and Kong.

—From a religious viewpoint the killing of Kong represents the killing of nature, and it is through nature that humans try to get closest to God. Kong was also the island natives' object of worship. He was everything to them. He was their god. When they lost him, they lost their reason for existence and their focus.

- Two subthemes in this film reflect certain fears of Americans. One is that civilization will cause us to lose our individuality, our identity and freedom. Another is the opposite, that we will have no laws, just chaos [disorganization]. A third is that we will lose control to the animal side of ourselves. Kong demonstrates that there is no place in our society for the animal. We fear our animal nature and must control it. We can't return to our primitive world, symbolized by Kong's island, and survive.

Film Noir as Genre

Film noir is a French term meaning "black film" or "dark film" and describes a type of Hollywood motion picture made in the postwar 1940s and into the 1950s. The setting is urban. The noir world is a dark and violent one of corruption and crime. The main characters are neurotic [mentally unstable] and amoral [unethical]. They are distanced from each other and can't find meaningful communication among themselves. The lighting is shadowy. There is a considerable contrast between light and darkness. The realism is heavy-handed [extremely real]. The tone is serious and heavy, the mood filled with tension and cynicism. Film noir roots [origins] include German Expressionism of the 1920s and the American gangster and detective genres of the 1930s (Konigsberg 1987, 122). Even today this film type survives in highly rated movies such as *Chinatown* (1974), *Body Heat* (1981), *Blood Simple* (1985), and *D.O.A.* (1988) (Telotte 1989, 3).

To quote Selby, author of *Dark City: The Film Noir*, "The *film noir* seems fundamentally about violations: vice, corruption, unrestrained desire, and most fundamental of all, abrogation [cancellation] of the American dream's most basic promises—of hope, prosperity, and safety from persecution" (Telotte 1989, 2).

Noir came into existence when it did for one big reason: World War Two ended. The return to normalcy was not a very satisfying one because of runaway inflation, labor disputes [arguments], unemployment, changes in the social status, and an increasing fear of a cold war with the Soviet Union. Americans' individual dreams and the well-known patterns of American life were being broken. The noir films illustrated this mood of disappointment and fear.

The film noir actually has literary origins that are, basically, the American and the English detective thriller novel. Authors of such include Dashiell Hammett, Raymond Chandler, Cornell Woolrich, and James M. Cain. Most particularly relevant is Hammett's protagonist Sam Spade of *The Maltese Falcon* and Chandler's character Philip Marlowe in, for example, *The Big Sleep* (Telotte 1989, 4–7).

The many films labeled film noir do not fit together neatly by way of common themes, characters, or plot but instead are grouped as such because of the tense and violent mood they generate [create] and because of the dark, cynical attitude they all have about life and human behavior. Basic to all of these films, however, is one of the following four storytelling patterns [strategies]:

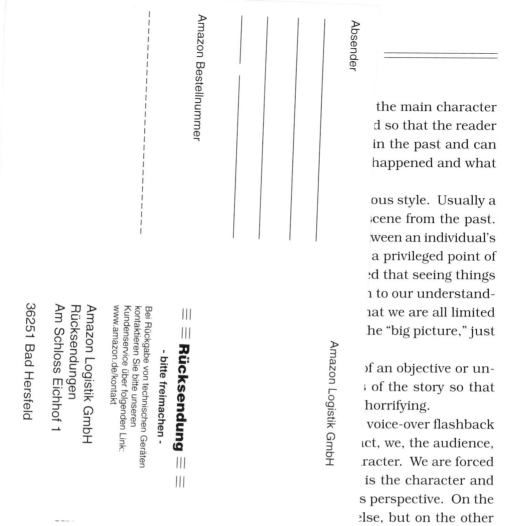

hand, we realize how much of our daily lives is unseen, hidden, and how incomplete our understanding of life is.

4. *The documentary style.* This was a technique that had become popular during World War Two, when so much publicity/propaganda from the war effort was brought to Americans on film. Many of the noir films, like the wartime documentaries, were shot on location, adding to the realistic effect. The United States was no different in this respect from other countries. Just after the war, every country's film industry returned to realism, probably because the war had broken all illusions (Telotte 1989, 12–22).

Often in the film noir there is the "black widow" character—a dishonest, dangerous, destructive female. *Double Indemnity* is a good example. It has been suggested that this character is a male fantasy and is symbolic of men's anxiety about the new and changing roles of women in postwar society. In these films such a woman is always destroyed, symbolizing the male's need to control her sexuality so that he will not be ruined by it. Having challenged the dominance of males in society, the woman must suffer.

In the noir world there is some sense of justice and equality. Generally both the law and the criminals are guilty. Both the individual and the society from which she or he came are to be blamed. And both seem to be searching through a violent world to find some sort of order and meaning (Telotte 1989, 33–34).

Previewing Questions
Laura

1. Like most film noir movies, the tone of this film is heavy, serious, and cynical. What are some of the ways in which this tone is expressed?
2. Notice the frequent focus of the camera on the portrait of Laura. What does the picture symbolize?

Laura

(1944) dir. Otto Preminger 88 min.
Starring: Gene Tierney, Dana Andrews, Clifton Webb

Setting: the big city

Characters

Laura Hunt [Gene Tierney]—a saleswoman in an advertisement firm. A kind, sweet, beautiful young woman.

Waldo Lydecker [Clifton Webb]—a famous writer/columnist. Very self-absorbed [egotistical]. He is a snob who is convinced he has the very best of taste. He admits that he is not a kind person but rather a vicious [mean] one, which, he believes, makes him charming in a different way.

Mark McPherson [Dana Andrews]—a policeman/detective of great integrity [honesty] and bravery. He is in charge of the investigation into the murder.

Shelby Carpenter [Vincent Price]—a playboy/gigolo of questionable finances. He used to live on income from his parents' estate in Kentucky until the money ran out. Then he lived off of rich friends, staying at their homes and borrowing money. Laura offers him a real job.

Anne Treadwell [Judith Anderson]—a rich aunt of Laura's. Shelby is having an affair with her, no doubt motivated by her money.

Plot

In Laura Hunt's apartment the police discover the body of a woman whose face has been destroyed by a gunshot. Naturally they assume Laura is the victim. Detective Mark McPherson is put in charge of the murder investigation. High on his list of suspects is Laura's dear friend, Waldo Lydecker. Waldo claims he's innocent and volunteers to help McPherson interview all the other suspects. Others on the list include Anne Treadwell and Shelby Carpenter. Waldo, apparently in a fit of jealousy, had told Laura that Anne and a young model named Diane Redfern were both dating Laura's fiancé, Shelby. When Laura finds out that this is true, she is very upset and goes to the country for a few days to decide what to do.

Meanwhile Laura returns from the country and seems to know nothing of the murder, although she is now a suspect herself. Even Shelby thinks she committed the murder, the victim being Diane Redfern and the motive being jealous revenge. Eventually McPherson arrests Laura, but in reality he suspects Waldo. When Laura is brought home from jail, Waldo is there to try to win her back to him again. When this fails, there is, in Waldo's mind, only one remaining course of action . . . .

Notes

- This film version was based upon the novel by Vera Caspary.

- *Laura* received an Oscar for best cinematography, and the theme song "Laura" was quite popular in its day.

- This film begins with a murder case and seems typical of the detective story/film genre except for one major difference: the detective Mark McPherson is obsessed not with the murderer but rather with the victim of the crime (Selby 1984, 24).

- In a way this is like George Bernard Shaw's play "Pygmalion." Waldo Lydecker, an art critic who thinks of himself as an expert on beauty, art, and good taste, decides to help Laura become sophisticated and successful. He sees her as his creation; she is his possession, the "abstract personification of his refined aesthetic ideals" (Selby 1984, 25). But he cannot make her love him, so he tries to destroy her, explaining, "When a man has everything he wants except what he wants most, he loses his self-respect. He becomes bitter and wants to hurt someone like he's been hurt" (25).

- Note that the portrait of Laura is the focus of both the beginning and the ending of the film. In the first half of the film this picture is very large, symbolizing the power and control this dream girl has over McPherson. However, when the real Laura appears, the portrait becomes smaller and melts [disappears] into the background. This is made very clear by the director in the scene in which Laura comes back to her apartment and we see her for the first time. At first Laura and McPherson stand facing each other with the portrait between them, as if McPherson were trying to decide whether to choose dream (the portrait) or reality (Laura herself). When she informs him of her decision not to marry Shelby, he makes his choice, steps toward her, and in so doing completely hides the portrait.

- Even after Laura has become "real," she is not easily won over romantically. She seems unavailable, unreachable, and McPherson and the audience are still hypnotized by her, still unsure of her. She is a puzzle, an enigma. We, like Mark, must determine her guilt or innocence (Selby 1984, 26).

Themes

- To McPherson, also, Laura is just an image, a kind of dream. When he first falls in love with her she is, he believes, already dead. She doesn't have to be alive to be the object of his love. The way Waldo and Mark feel about her is illustrative of the film's main theme: we, the audience, should question any kind of aesthetic [cerebral rather than physical] love that doesn't need its human object to be alive. The dream of Laura comes true for Mark McPherson only because he can ignore the dream Laura (as represented by her portrait), while Waldo loves only the dream, the Laura he "created" (Selby 1984, 25).

- Another theme is the cultural deterioration [destruction], the moral decay [ruin] of the upper class, symbolized by Waldo. Like him, other members of this class, such as Anne Treadwell and Shelby Carpenter, also lack the capacity to love someone. They are empty, impotent [powerless], selfish characters interested only in acquiring more status and status symbols. These characters are self-centered and think of themselves as better than everyone else.

The Western Genre

Most film critics agree that there is not one particular formula that every western follows. An especially well-known one is, however, that in which (*a*) a conflict arises in the town; (*b*) the protagonist, or hero, determines, on peril [danger] of death, to end this conflict (which usually involves one or more outlaws); (*c*) order and civilization cannot be restored until, with the hero's help, the threat [danger] from these bad guys is eliminated. The hero doesn't have to be an outsider; in some films he is already a member of the community. It is also not true in every western that the boy gets the girl. He sometimes aids the community and then moves on. In those westerns in which romance is central, the hero may be injured [hurt] but he doesn't usually die. In another type of formula western the hero is an unwilling one. He is not originally a "good" man but is transformed [changed] by events around him and becomes a hero. This type often dies in the end, redeemed [saved] but still dead (Tuska 1985, 20).

Other typical western plots include stories about building railroads, telegraphs, stagecoach routes; or about long trips such as cattle drives or wagon trains. In this type the villains [bad guys] attempt to prevent these goals from being achieved. Another type of western has a wandering hero who moves aimlessly [without destination] from place to place looking for adventure or who is searching for something or someone. Yet another type revolves around a ranch, and the conflict concerns a small group who wants to take over the ranch or steal the livestock (Tuska 1985, 24–27). Other western protagonists are out for revenge. Either the hero must right a wrong done to him or the bad guy tries to get revenge for what the hero has done to him. In both cases the men usually act outside the law to accomplish their own special kind of justice. Another western type has Indians at the center of the story. Usually these Indians are seen as malevolent [bad], and any white woman taken by them dies or loses her place in white society, and any Indian woman who marries a white man will generally die by film's end. The hero who is forced to become an outlaw [a lawless person] is the subject of yet another kind of plot. This "good badman" is usually a sympathetic character whose problems are psychological, brought about by an unhappy past. A final western type concerns marshals, sheriffs, rangers, and deputies, i.e., lawmen. This lawman type was then placed into one of the previously mentioned plots, especially those concerning revenge, outlaws, ranches, or Indians. In fact most of these occur in combination rather than in their pure forms (29–37). *High Noon*, for instance, is a combination of the romantic western and the lawman plot.

Previewing Questions
High Noon

1. Review the section that explains the western genre. What type of formula western, or what combination of types, is *High Noon*?
2. Listen carefully to the words and music of the ballad being sung by Tex Ritter in the opening scenes and in other scenes throughout the film. What function does this song serve?

High Noon

(1952) dir. Fred Zinnemann 85 min.
Starring: Gary Cooper, Grace Kelly

Setting: 10:40 A.M., the small town of Hadleyville, in a western territory. (This is one of the few Hollywood films that does NOT condense time. Instead, after the early scenes, screen time conforms to real time.)

Characters

Will Cane [Gary Cooper]—the retiring marshal of Hadleyville. [Cooper won his second Best Actor Oscar for this role.]

Amy [Grace Kelly]—a young Quaker woman. Quakers don't believe in violence and killing, so Will promises to give up being a marshal after they marry.

Harvey Pell [Lloyd Bridges]—the deputy marshal. He is angry because the town government didn't choose him to replace Will Cane as marshal. Instead, they chose to bring in a new man from out of town. Harve thinks that Will is jealous of him because he (Harve) won the girl, Helen Ramirez, whom both of them had been dating.

Helen Ramirez [Katy Jurado]—a Mexican widow who owns a store in town. She was in love with Will, but he left her, so she started seeing Harvey. She was also the girlfriend of Frank Miller five years ago. She's the stereotypical "bad" girl with a heart of gold. Only a "pure" woman can win the man in Hollywood westerns.

Plot

This is a western classic, the story of a brave lawman who, on his wedding day, has to face outlaws who have sworn to kill him. The leader of the badmen, Frank Miller, is supposed to arrive on the noon train. Then there will be a showdown [a shooting match in the streets]. These men want to kill Will because five years before, Marshal Cane had arrested Frank Miller and Miller was supposed to hang; but the judge let him out of jail after five years and now he and his brother Ben and friends are coming back to get revenge. The words of the ballad at the beginning of the film tell the story. The narrator of the song, a famous cowboy singer named Tex Ritter, is worried not only about the men coming to kill him but also about losing his new wife, who wants to leave him rather than stay and see him shot dead by the outlaws.

Notes

- *High Noon* follows the basic formula of many romance westerns in that there is a hero, Will Cane; a conflict, with the Miller gang; and the danger of the hero's dying to end the conflict. Cane's heroic attempts are, ironically, not appreciated by the town. The townspeople believe that by staying in town to face the Miller gang, Cane is placing everyone in jeopardy [danger] because the Millers want revenge on Cane for putting them in jail. In fact, in the townspeople's opinion, Cane is inviting an end to order and civilization by staying in town. The lawman's value to the community seems to be limited. Cane also almost loses the girl, his wife, because of his determination to stop the outlaws all by himself, whereas usually the hero wins the girl. *High Noon* thus follows, at least partially, three western formulas: the romance western, the lawman plot, and the revenge motif. It is a particularly good example of the lawman type of western because it ends with a climactic shoot-out.

- From about 1900 to 1975 many young American men went to the Saturday matinees to see the westerns. Cowboy stars included Roy Rogers, Tom Mix, Lash LaRue, and Gene Autry. Many of these men were singing cowboys. Western radio shows were popular in the 1930s and 1940s, and later, in the 1950s and 1960s, TV cowboy shows were popular. In 1959, thirty-five western shows were aired weekly on TV, and eight of the top ten TV programs were westerns. John Wayne, symbolic in America of all that is masculine, was in many westerns (and war films). Western novels and short stories have been well liked throughout the twentieth century. Well-known writers include Zane Grey, Ernest Haycox, Max Brand, Luke Short, and Louis L'Amour. (Louis L'Amour books numbered 145 million in 1984 [Tompkins 1992, 5].) The western novel provided, for men, a model for themselves. In fact, from a feminist point of view, it can be said that westerns make women see themselves as men do. Women are often merely sex objects and housekeepers (17).

- The western is antithetical [opposite] to love and order, which women believe in, so therefore the opinions of women are unimportant. Religion, which also represents structure, order, and peace, is also ignored in the westerns. Western men had their own separate code: the law of the West, celebrating violence as heroism. The tough western man enjoyed physical challenges and punishments. They preferred the company of each other to that of women. Like the churches, they had their own rituals, including the duel, or gunfight. The gun was their idol (Tompkins 1992, 10–14).

- Women in western films are not, in themselves, important. The girl, or heroine, is there just to cause love or fear or in some way to get a reaction from the hero. She is a kind of plot device [tool] rather than a fully developed, complicated character (Tuska 1985, 224). Not only are women colorless and predictable in their limited roles in westerns but they are also "masculinized" because they accept the nature of violence. Sometimes they are even violent themselves, indicating that violence is the best problem solver (229). This can be seen in Amy Cane's behavior in the final scenes.

- Amy swears that if her husband has a gunfight with Frank Miller, she will leave him. Very often this scenario is played in the western. The man must protect his honor and, to show that he is not controlled by his woman, he must reject her pleas and do exactly the opposite of what she has asked. Frequently in these films the women don't leave after all; they come back to their men, so the men never have to worry.

- Sheriff Will Cane's face is twisted into a pained expression throughout the film. He is disgusted with the world and the awful men in it (Tuska 1985, 219). He had been attempting to escape that world, to marry and settle down. He hates having to do what could get him killed and what is so unpleasant for his wife. As she says, "I don't care who's right or who's wrong. There has to be some better way for people to live!" (227). But the hurt on his face is also mixed with determination. It's a heavy responsibility, but he must act like a man and protect the town rather than run away with his bride. To this extent Will Cane is the typical western hero. Separating him from the bad guys is the fact that he still has feelings. But as a tough guy, Cane must hide his true feelings. The villains, by contrast, are simply brutal [mean] and without morals (219).

- Part of the western film's pattern is that before the big showdown, the hero has a smaller fight with a minor character. This is to prove his moral superiority and to get the audience on his side. Another part of the pattern is that the action must build so much suspense that finally the hero has no choice: he must act, he must retaliate [get revenge] with violence. There's a point at which the audience feels relief from the tensions that were building between the hero and the bad guys. By the time the hero reacts violently and kills someone, we, the audience, have seen clearly that he was victimized and that he has the moral right to kill. We applaud [clap for] the murders (Tuska 1985, 228).

- Director Zinnemann builds our sense of excitement and our identification with the characters through his masterful camera work. For instance, in the climactic scene of this film, the camera starts with a close-up on Will Cane, then rises to include the empty street. The camera focuses only on him as he walks down this lonely street on his way to face the villains at the railroad station. The long walk and our knowledge of his emotional state work together to make this a very moving [emotional, exciting] scene. Cane is alone, without friends and support, facing death at "high noon" (Knight 1957, 187).

- This film contains certain symbolic elements that make it almost allegorical [representative of abstract or spiritual meaning conveyed through physical or concrete forms]:
  —The Miller Gang = chaos, violence, barbarism.
  —Will Cane = the transition [change, transformation] figure. He is the bridge from violent chaos to civilization. He represents law and order, but to keep order he must carry a gun and kill.
  —Amy = the symbol of civilization, family, moral values.
  —The train = the tool by which civilization is able to move westward.

Themes

- Law and Order are superior to Chaos.

- Civilization must win against Lawlessness and Violence.

- The "wild" West must be transformed into orderly, civilized communities.

- A quote from one of the characters probably best summarizes the film's most important message about the uselessness of violence and the need for civilized ways: "In the end you end up dyin' all alone on a dirty street. And for what? For nothin' " (Tompkins 1992, 50).

Comedy as Genre

Laughter has a healing effect. In times of trauma, grief, and loss, people need to be reminded of the silly side of life and of their own foolish behavior. The common person is more often a fool than a tragic hero. From the very beginning of film history, comedy has been a popular genre. The earliest short-reel, silent films were often comedies. Charlie Chaplin is among the earliest and best-known silent comedians. His best works include *The Tramp* (1915) and *The Gold Rush* (1925) (Sennett 1992, 1–3). Slapstick, or visual jokes, like falls off of buildings or pies in the face, was a key ingredient in early comedy.

When sound pictures became more numerous in the 1930s, more emphasis was placed on witty [humorous] dialogue. Fast-paced, sophisticated comedies about the rich became popular. Additionally, the screwball or romantic comedy was born. (See the chapter entitled "Aspects of the Romantic Comedy.") On the other hand, slapstick and absurdity didn't die. There were "clowns" of film in their own special movies, too. These stars included Mae West (*She Done Him Wrong*, 1933), the Marx Brothers (*A Night at the Opera*, 1935), Stan Laurel and Oliver Hardy (*Way Out West*, 1937), and W. C. Fields, (*The Bank Dick*, 1940), all of whom had a special style and identifiable dress. These comic figures in their foolish roles helped the American people to forget the tragedy, poverty, and hopelessness of the Great Depression of 1929–40 (Sennett 1992, 53).

By the early 1940s World War Two had begun in Europe and the United States had just entered the fight. At this point came "the democratization of American comedy." Comedians began to look like normal people, to be soldiers or salespeople or any average American citizen. The difference was in their behavior. In attempting to deal with a crisis, they were always awkward and incompetent; i.e., no matter how hard they tried, they always stupidly failed. Examples include Bud Abbott and Lou Costello (*Buck Privates*, 1941), Danny Kaye (*Up In Arms*, 1944), and Red Skelton (*A Southern Yankee*, 1948) (Sennett 1992, 98–104).

Because men were away at war, women began to have more responsible roles in the workplace, and in comedy female characters were aggressive, working women. Yet in the end they always had to give up their careers in order to get and keep a man. This attitude, even in comedy, that a woman's place is in the home, would not change for thirty or more years (Sennett 1992, 116).

After World War Two, from about 1945 until the early 1950s, comedies became more domestic: the subjects were home and family and the crises experienced there. The American dream, not the real world, was portrayed. Filmgoers needed a feeling of security and order in their lives after the hardship of the war. Such films included *Sitting Pretty* (1948), from which a television series, *Mr. Belvedere*, would come almost forty years later, and *Father of the Bride* (1950), remade in 1991 (Sennett 1992, 152–55).

Finally in the 1960s comedy would change. In particular, romantic comedies became more openly sexual. And other risqué [shocking] topics also became subjects for movies. Satires [movies that ridicule and make fun] of sex, marriage, advertising, and money were plentiful [many]. These included *Boys' Night Out* (1962), *Lover Come Back* (1962), and *Sex and The Single Girl* (1964) (Sennett 1992, 196–200). The subject of infidelity [being unfaithful to a spouse] was an especially popular subject: *Good Neighbor Sam* (1964), *Guide for the Married Man* (1967), *Divorce, American Style* (1967), and *The Secret Life of an American Wife* (1968) (209–11).

Other subjects were also satirized. In fact any topic could be ridiculed, from death (*The Loved One*, 1965) to war (*Dr. Strangelove or: How I Learned to Stop Worrying and Love the Bomb*, 1964) to Jewish suburban life (*Goodbye, Columbus*, 1969) to social alienation (*The Graduate*, 1967) (Sennett 1992, 218–22).

As the 1970s arrived, the social climate in the United States was changing rapidly. There was a spirit of "antiestablishment rebellion" [protest against the status quo, or state of being, especially the government and social organizations]. New kinds of romance were being experimented with in comedy. For instance, in *Harold and Maude* (1971), an eighty-year-old woman and a twenty-year-old boy have a romantic relationship. The stereotypical romantic character was changed too. Instead of a woman with a classic, beautiful face and figure, the lead character could be someone like Barbra Streisand, with imperfect features and a Brooklyn accent. Other films about odd couples and strange romances included: *Made For Each Other* (1971), *Butterflies are Free* (1972), and *10* (1979) (Sennett 1992, 236–43).

With the 1980s came the idea that a career for women could be just as significant as love and could even be combined with love. It was also made clear that love could take many forms other than romantic: *Broadcast News* (1987), *Working Girl* (1988), and *When Harry Met Sally* (1989). Comedies about marriage and divorce, in contrast, got darker and more negative: *The War of the Roses* (1989).

On the other hand, the joys of being a parent were very evident in the comic films of the 1980s. The idea seemed to be to make adults (especially men) less selfish and self-centered and to bring them back into the traditional family environment, as in *Baby Boom* (1987), *Raising Arizona* (1987), *Three Men and a Baby* (1987), and *Look Who's Talking* (1989) (Sennett 1992, 278–95).

In the 1990s comedy continues to use satire to ridicule the social norms of the day, although in recent years there has been a return to family values and a less adventurous spirit in the action and dialogue. The truly great directors of satire are a part of the past. Among the greatest were Preston Sturges (*The Lady Eve*, 1941), Ernst Lubitsch (*To Be or Not to Be*, 1942), and Billy Wilder (*Some Like It Hot*, 1959) (Scheuer 1985, 809–10).

Previewing Questions
Some Like It Hot

1. How does this film parody [make fun of] gangsters and gangster films?
2. Joe and Jerry each experience a personality transformation when they become girls in the band. How is each one changed? Are the changes positive?

Some Like It Hot

(1959) dir. Billy Wilder   122 min.
Starring: Tony Curtis, Jack Lemmon, Marilyn Monroe

Setting: the Jazz Age of the 1920s, Chicago, Illinois; later setting: Miami, Florida, the Seminole-Ritz Hotel

Characters

Joe (Josephine) [Tony Curtis]—always irresponsible. He spends all his money and Jerry's on gambling and women. He uses his charm to get what he wants.

Jerry (Daphne) [Jack Lemmon]—very tolerant of his friend Joe's silly ideas. Joe is always able to convince [persuade] Jerry to do what he wants him to do. Consequently they never have any money and they owe everyone.

Sugar Kane [Marilyn Monroe]—a problem drinker who also has problems with men. She tends to fall in love often with irresponsible musicians, especially saxophone players, who later leave her with "the fuzzy end of the lollipop" [with nothing].

Spats Columbo [George Raft]—the leader of the mob [Mafia] that murders the other mob members. He owns the speakeasy [bar] that gets raided [attacked] at the beginning of the film. He always wears spats over his shoes, hence his nickname.

Osgood Fielding, III [Joe E. Brown]—the millionaire with the yacht [luxury boat]. He falls in love with Daphne.

Plot

Joe, a saxophone player, and Jerry, a bass player, are two unemployed musicians who accidentally witness [see] a mass murder of one mob by another gang of mobsters. The gang wants to murder the two musicians before they can tell the police what they saw and who did it. The two men have no money and no car, but they need to get out of town. When they find out that a traveling all-girls' band is looking for a sax and a bass player, they decide to dress up like girls and take the job, thereby escaping from the gangsters. The story line revolves around how much difficulty they have in playing the role of women.

Notes

- The title *Some Like It Hot* is a reference to jazz, which is a lively, complex style of music that reflects the wild behavior of the main characters of this film. The lyrics [words] of the theme song, sung by Sugar, mirror the philosophy of the time, which spoke of being wild, reckless, and carefree.

- The setting of this film is the Jazz Age (note the music) and the Prohibition Era. In l9l9 the Volstead Act was passed defining alcoholic drinks. In l920 the Eighteenth Amendment to the U.S. Constitution was passed prohibiting the sale and manufacture of alcoholic beverages. (It was an unpopular law, repealed in l933.) During Prohibition many bars, called "speakeasies," opened up secretly to sell alcohol. The alcohol was manufactured illegally by bootleggers. The Mafia found that selling liquor illegally and owning speakeasies was big business, so they got very involved. Sometimes people got killed, either by police or by interfering competitive Mafia men. Sometimes there were raids by the police on these secret bars.

- The first scenes are set in Chicago during the Prohibition Era, at the time of the St. Valentine's Day Massacre. On this bloody day, February 14, l929, seven unarmed bootlegging gang members were murdered in Chicago. The fight concerned control of the illegal liquor traffic in Chicago. Al Capone's gang, dressed as cops [police], lined up "Bugs" Moran's gang against the wall of a garage and shot them down.

- Joe and Jerry are transformed [changed] by their experience as women. As a man, Joe is a womanizer who merely exploits women, using them and then leaving them. As a woman, he learns to be sympathetic and sincere. His friendship with Sugar shows him how poorly she has been treated by men. When, in the final scenes, he walks up in drag [in women's clothing] and kisses her, telling her that no man is worth her tears, we see that he has learned how to love, that he has finally understood how men can hurt women. Jerry, too, is changed. Having always before been in the shadow of good-looking Joe, he now becomes more self-confident. He believes he is attractive. Unbelievably he begins to even think of himself as a woman, and since Osgood doesn't seem to mind the truth, it seems that Jerry may actually become a woman (Bell-Metereau 1985, 54–56).

- There are ironies in this role reversal. For instance, as a woman, Joe acts like a man with Sugar, giving her advice and protecting her. However, when Joe is the male millionaire, Sugar becomes the aggressor and he is submissive and shy. It is also interesting that Joe, who is more masculine than Jerry, actually looks more feminine as a woman than does Jerry, who in reality is the more effeminate [feminine] one of the two men. A further irony is that Jerry, who is submissive to Joe in real life, gets to be more dominant and aggressive as a woman. When he is with Osgood, he is in control, even to the point of leading when they dance (Bell-Metereau 1985, 58–59).

- When the Mafia gather at the hotel in Miami they call themselves "Friends of the Italian Opera." This title is a joke in several ways. First, an illegal organization cannot openly meet under its real name. Second, it seems ridiculous and out of character for murderous, dishonest men to be opera lovers. And last, the Mafia's origins are Italy and Sicily.

- Director Billy Wilder shot this picture in black and white rather than color for two reasons. One was to make the 1920s set look more authentic [real]. The other was to cover the ugly makeup of Curtis and Lemmon. They both looked horrible in color because of the heavy makeup they had to wear. Besides, in color, if the makeup were too lightly applied, the men would look not like women but like transvestites, and if it were applied too heavily, they would seem vulgar (Bell-Metereau 1985, 55).

- The shooting of the film was also a problem because of Marilyn Monroe. She was always late and often in a bad mood. One scene had to be done fifty-nine times before she remembered her lines correctly. Tony Curtis said that kissing her was like kissing Hitler. The experience was so bad that Wilder decided never to work with her again. (This was his second film with her; the first was *The Seven-Year Itch*.) Half jokingly he told one interviewer: "I have discussed this [the filming] with my doctor and my psychiatrist and they tell me I'm too old and too rich to go through this again" (Madsen 1969, 114–18).

- Wilder is among Hollywood's finest directors. His films are humorous, realistic, and sarcastic. Like Hitchcock, he is considered an auteur, being an excellent scriptwriter and director. Unlike Hitchcock, Wilder didn't confine himself to one genre. He directed comedies, drama, and even film noir. Some of his best films include *Double Indemnity* (1944), *Sunset Boulevard* (1950), *Stalag 17* (1953), *The Seven-Year Itch* (1955), *The Apartment* (1960), and *Irma La Douce* (1963).

Themes

- *Some Like It Hot* is a parody [makes fun] of gangster films, even to the point of including the infamous St. Valentine's Day Massacre. The gangsters are associated with death. In fact, the opening scene contains a hearse and a coffin, and the speakeasy is inside a funeral home.

To further emphasize the violent nature of the gangsters, director Wilder includes another massacre later in Florida. At the "convention," a machine gunner comes out of a huge cake to murder the guests of honor in order to get revenge for Spats's having rubbed out [killed] Toothpick Charlie. The film makes fun of other aspects of Mafia life besides their concepts of violence and revenge. For instance, the gangsters all have nicknames, and the majority of them, except for their leaders who are cool and calm, are portrayed as extremely stupid and excitable.

- The director also parodies sexual stereotypes. As men, Joe and Jerry are definite male "types." Joe is sexy and macho, smooth with women, while Jerry is weak and indecisive. But as women the roles are reversed as Joe becomes soft, sweet, flirtatious and Jerry becomes more outgoing, popular, and even aggressive—a party "girl." Marilyn Monroe's character is the stereotype of the sweet, sexy, dumb blonde. She's so "sweet" that her name is Sugar Kane. Joe also pretends to be a rich, high society yachtsman in yet another stereotype. Osgood Fielding is the stereotype of the rich, dirty old man, giving the traditional gifts of flowers and jewelry. The implication seems to be that stereotypes are destructive. They disrupt [interfere with] the lives and loves of everyone. This is clear from the song "I'm Through With Love" that the brokenhearted Sugar sings.

- A homosexual theme is strongly suggested, especially in the way in which Joe and Jerry transform themselves. They wear makeup, high heels, and dresses, and they study the women around them carefully so that their imitation will be a good one. They seem very enthusiastic about becoming women, and after a while they begin to talk and think like women as they discuss life and men with each other (Bell-Metereau 1985, 56–57). There are other indications on a covert [hidden] level that there is a homosexual bond between the two of them. Reference is made at least four times to the fact that they both have type "O" blood. This blood type is the universal donor for all other blood types and could be a subtle way of stating that Joe and Jerry are either homosexual or, more likely, bisexual. There are, perhaps, five references to the "fuzzy end of the lollipop," which is an idiomatic expression denoting a bad situation, but which in sexual terms could refer to fellatio [oral stimulation to the penis]. Further, while Sugar tries to excite Joe, he complains that women are not attractive to him and that Nature has made an exception of him. The last and most obvious example is in the last scene, when Osgood assures Jerry that he doesn't care that Jerry is really a man disguised as a woman.

Chapter 3
Feminism and the Feminist Film

Feminism has to do with the changing role of women and how they view themselves. It is "a redefinition of women . . . and what they can do, how they feel, and how forcefully they transcend traditional definitions of who they are and should be" (Jameson 1994, 278). In other words, feminism is a reaction against a society that is seen to be male-dominated, and in which women are, in many respects, treated like second-class citizens.

Consideration of equal rights for women was neglected for centuries. Occasionally someone, usually female, took issue. For example, in 1792 the Anglo-Irish woman Mary Wollstonecraft published *A Vindication of the Rights of Women* in which she challenged the notion that women's major function was to please men. In her work she suggested equal opportunities for women in education, work, and politics (*Encyclopaedia Britannica*, 15th ed., s. v. "Women's liberation movement"). She further asserted that the same standards of morality should apply to both sexes: men believed that they didn't have to follow certain standards, such as marital fidelity.

Finally with the passage of the Nineteenth Amendment to the U.S. Constitution, women earned the right to vote. In the 1920s women had become freer in their behavior. They could drive cars, smoke cigarettes, and wear whatever clothing they wished. More and more women went to college to learn professions. Yet the status quo didn't change for them. Men were still paid more, as they are today, for the same types of jobs. (The belief was that since women were supposed to be married, they didn't need equal salaries because their husbands would support them.) For a while prior to and during World War Two droves [thousands] of women

40

entered the work force. However, the postwar era was notoriously [infamously] antifeminist. After men returned from the battlefields, women were expected to give up their jobs and quietly return home to the kitchen and the bedroom. In the 1950s it was unthinkable for women to seek [look for] self-fulfillment, except through marriage and family. Single women were viewed at best as strange, and at worst, as promiscuous [sexually impure].

The Women's Liberation Movement, a powerful social and political force, was probably born in 1963 with the publication of Betty Friedan's book, *The Feminine Mystique*. Throughout the decade of the 1970s, in fact, there was vast [much] upheaval and rejection of the norms and values of the "establishment," that is, the government and anyone over the age of thirty. Social change brought with it sexual revolution, and with the advent [coming] of the birth-control pill, women were liberated from the possibility of unwanted pregnancy. The most famous spokeswomen of women's rights and freedom were (and continue to be) Ms. Friedan, Germaine Greer, and Gloria Steinem, who have argued that feminists are neither masculine aberrations [male freaks] nor men haters because they choose to challenge traditional behaviors and beliefs.

Due to the influence of both the women's movement and economic uncertainty brought about by the debts incurred [caused by] the Vietnam War and other political issues, more and more single and married women found themselves in the workplace in the 1970s. This decade was thus distinguished by the attention given to job equality.

The decade of the 1980s saw a more conservative government and society offended by the "radical" idea of female equality, so a united women's movement went underground. In its place two factions [sides] emerged whose proponents [supporters] were thought of as either feminine or feminist. A woman could not be both. The 1980s also gave rise to violent demonstrations for and against a woman's right to reproductive freedom. Additionally, although long-contributing members of the work force, women continued to be faced with job and salary inequities [injustices] and sexual harassment.

Currently the feminist agenda [program] includes not only those issues of the past, but also those having to do with domestic violence, child care, child abuse, racism, homophobia [fear and hatred of homosexuals], and women's health, to name a few. In other words, feminism encompasses [includes] the larger, human questions of self-determination and freedom.

Feminist film, as is true of feminism itself, must be viewed within a larger historical framework, and unlike other genres in this textbook that can be described formally, deals with emotional themes that have arisen out of the "urgency of the time[s]" (Jameson 1994, 278).

As we have seen, the 1920s figure prominently in the history of feminism. Women had won the right to vote, and their influence had spread, even to the movies: "more women worked as screenwriters in the twenties and thirties than at any time before or since" (Keough 1994, 280). In the 1930s women, like film itself, had found their voice, and female passion and sexuality were expressed freely and aggressively by such famous stars as Marlene Dietrich, Mae West, and Jean Harlow. But, as is always the case in history, backlash [reaction] set in; this time, in the guise [appearance] of the Hays Production Code, which sought to promote social respectability and decency.

Although blatant [clearly expressed] sexuality was suppressed [put down], strong women like Katharine Hepburn, Barbara Stanwyck, Bette Davis, and Joan Crawford continued to hold their own. The so-called women's pictures of the 1930s and 1940s were successful "because they featured complex and strong female characters confronting issues that leave guys cold [don't interest men]—things like mature sexual relationships, the conflict between one's nature and one's social role, the pressures of family, and the specter [presence] of mortality" (Keough 1994, 280–81).

As was true in real life, women in the films of the 1950s were dehumanized, for the most part, and, perhaps strangely, the perception of women and their role in society deteriorated [fell apart] even further in the permissive [free] 1960s. There were two major reasons for this phenomenon. The first was the dissolving of the production code into a ratings system that allowed sex, nudity, and violence to be shown on the movie screen, just as long as children were not witness to them. The second reason was male-dominated Hollywood, which saw film as the vehicle [way] by which men could escape from and have their frustrations vented against women who, by the 1970s, had pushed themselves into traditional male arenas [aspects] of American life (Keough 1994, 282).

Misogyny [hatred of women] in film can be clearly seen in the past two decades, especially in those films that promote woman as victim or sex object. As was the case of the post–World War Two era when tradition threatened to unravel [come apart], the early stirrings of feminism were crushed quickly and completely. More insidious [frightening], however, is conscious or unconscious intent on the part of contemporary filmmakers to direct the anger that women feel, not against an unequal system, but against themselves. Examples of films in which women bash women include *The Hand That Rocks the Cradle* and *Death Becomes Her*, both released the year after the enormously popular and feministically acclaimed

Thelma and Louise (1991). Further, one can point to few truly positive characteristics that underlie feminist film. While it is true that all feminist protagonists are strong and independent, none seem able to overcome social, sexual, or financial inequality without reverting to [going back to] traditionally held views of female inferiority and male superiority. The hope is that "once Hollywood recognizes women as human, it will also have to acknowledge the human qualities of understanding, compassion, commitment, and love" (Keough 1994, 283).

Previewing Questions
Pat and Mike

1. Read the section entitled "Feminism and the Feminist Film." In what ways is the female lead, Pat, a product of the 1950s? In what ways does she embody more contemporary feminist values?
2. *Pat and Mike* raises the issues of possessions and possessiveness. Who is possessed by whom?

Pat and Mike

(1952) dir. George Cukor 95 min.
Starring: Katharine Hepburn, Spencer Tracy, William Ching

Setting: the West Coast; New York City; the tour circuit

Characters

Collier Weld [William Ching]—assistant administrative vice president at Pacific Tech.

Mrs. Pat Pemberton [Katharine Hepburn]—a widow, engaged to Collier. She works at Pacific Tech. as a physical education instructor.

Mike Conovan [Spencer Tracy]—a sports promoter. He is a rough character who speaks "left-handed" [bad, ungrammatical] English.

Davie Hucko [Aldo Ray]—a professional boxer who keeps losing his bouts [matches]. He is very dumb.

Plot

Initial scenes of the film introduce the conflict between Pat and Collier. The golf match with the Bemingers serves to show that Collier's shaky [less than complete] belief in Pat's ability makes her unable to do her best when he is around her. He is not supportive of her; instead, he makes her doubt herself. Collier's only desire is to impress the Bemingers because he is a fund-raiser for the college, and they have a lot of money that could be donated. Mrs. Beminger has an especially irritating personality and she gives Pat, who is a much better golfer, useless advice about how to improve her golf game. At game's end, Pat turns angrily on Mrs. Beminger, but in reality it is her fiancé, Collier, with whom she is irritated.

At the country club where Pat and Collier play is a golf pro [a person that makes a living playing sports] who decides Pat should enter a big golf tournament, so she quits her job at Pacific Tech. While at the tournament, she meets Mike Conovan, who wants her to "throw" [lose] the match because he and his crooked [dishonest] "business associates" have bets on another golfer. Pat refuses, but she does decide to keep his business card. Unlike Collier, Mike appreciates her abilities, and the scenes with him are meant to show a contrast between Mike's and Collier's attitudes toward Pat. Mike respects her talents and even offers her a contract to be a professional athlete. Collier, on the other hand, just wants Pat to be his wife.

The outcome of the golf match and Collier's general attitude toward Pat cause her to decide that she has to prove to him, as well as to herself, that she is not a failure, and that she needs to be dependent only on herself.

Pat goes to see Mike in order to accept his offer to give her a contract as a professional athlete whom he will train and promote in both golf and tennis. There she meets Davie Hucko, a boxer who keeps losing all of his bouts [matches] and another one of Mike's protégés [people whom someone trains and protects]. Mike manipulates [controls] Hucko by asking him the "Three Big Questions": Who made you? Who owns the biggest piece of you? What'll happen if I drop you? On the other hand, Mike is lucky to have Pat to promote: he sees her as a financial asset, and he wants her to consider herself to be his equal partner. Just before a tennis match to be held at her home college of Pacific Tech, Mike tells Pat that she is beautiful. Unfortunately for her, Collier shows up at the match and ruins her game.

Afterward in the locker room, Mike and Collier start arguing about who owns her. She objects, crying out that no one owns her. This philosophy also extends to Hucko: Pat tells him that the person he has to beat is himself. Her talk with him is successful: Hucko wins his next fight.

Mike's "business associates," who are really crooks and gamblers, come by to ask him how to bet on a golf match that Pat will be in. Mike refuses to "throw" the game because he has learned from Pat how to be honest. Pat, too, is transformed [changed] by her relationship with Mike because she has become more self-assured. Later there is a fight and Pat protects Mike from the attackers. He is insulted by her action, believing that fighting is something that only men do and that therefore she has taken away his masculinity by protecting him. However, the roles are reversed when Collier appears and Mike "protects" Pat from him. Thus we see that their relationship is an equal one, which is based on mutual concern and respect.

Notes

- George Cukor, the "woman's director," was very pro-female. His sympathy toward women and women's issues is evident not only in this film but also in some of his other classics such as *Little Women* (1933), *Sylvia Scarlett* (1936), *The Women* (1939), and *Adam's Rib* (1949).

- *Pat and Mike* is believable because the main female character, Pat, is not typically feminine. Her clothing, her hair, her sports prowess [skill], and even her name, which can be either male or female, indicate that she is not the stereotypical submissive female. It should be noted, however, that her so-called masculine qualities suggest that the level of her independence and that the equality that she gains can only be reached by women who possess male traits [characteristics].

- Unlike Hucko, whom Mike keeps under control by asking the "Three Big Questions," and unlike Little Nell, the racehorse, Pat is owned by no one.

Themes

- This film is hopeful in tone, indicating by way of the relationship between Pat and Mike that equality and respect of one sex for the other are possible. Considering that *Pat and Mike* was made in 1952, when a woman's place was in the home, caring for husband and children, this feminist theme is surprising.

- As is true in the case of more current feminist films, the female lead in *Pat and Mike* is tough and independent. Conversely, however, there is no supportive group of women from whom Pat can gain strength. This is perhaps due to historical context because the post–World War Two era in Hollywood was very conservative. "The boys [soldiers] had marched home for good, and the women who remained behind on the screen found their roles increasingly delimited [limited, defined]" (Keough 1994, 282). One can only assume that it was the strength of Katharine Hepburn's character in real life and her vast appeal to movie audiences that permitted her to receive less insipid [flat, boring] roles than her female contemporaries. More commonly, powerful women were "quashed [crushed] swiftly and thoroughly" (282).

Previewing Questions
9 to 5

1. The film focuses on several inequities that women face in the workplace. What are they? Are they resolved?
2. What is *empowerment*? Do the three female leads empower themselves by the end of the film? If so, how?
3. In what ways is Frank Hart the stereotypical "male chauvinist pig"? Do you think that Frank Hart could exist in real life?

9 to 5

(1980) dir. Colin Higgins 111 min.
Starring: Jane Fonda, Lily Tomlin, Dolly Parton, Dabney Coleman

Setting: the big city

Characters

Judy Burnly [Jane Fonda]—a housewife, soon to be divorced, because her husband wants to marry his secretary.

Violet Newstead [Lily Tomlin]—a widow with four children. She is very bright and competent. Although she has been with the company for twelve years, she still holds only a relatively low administrative position.

Doralee Rhodes [Dolly Parton]—Hart's secretary. She is sweet and kind and happily married, but Hart is always trying to seduce her.

Frank Hart [Dabney Coleman]—the boss. Violet trained him and he was quickly promoted, while Violet, who is superior to him in work skills, remains in lower management. The three women refer to Hart as a "sexist, egotistical [self-centered], lying, hypocritical [insincere] bigot [racist]."

Plot

Judy, insecure and inexperienced, comes for her first day of work. Gradually, and with Violet's help, Judy improves her office skills. Meanwhile, Violet has been waiting for a promotion from Mr. Hart, which is, instead, given to an inexperienced young man. Violet is enraged [extremely angry]. Doralee is also angry with Hart when she discovers that he has been telling everyone in the office that he's having an affair with her. Judy, too, is furious when she finds out that Maria Delgado, a Hispanic employee, has been fired for no good reason. The three women—Judy, Violet, and Doralee—are thus brought together by their mutual dislike of their boss. This bond is strengthened one night after they get drunk and smoke marijuana together. Each shares her fantasy with the others about how she would get rid of Hart.

Judy's fantasy is first. In her "dream," everyone in the office is hunting Hart down as if he were an escaped prisoner or a wild animal.

Doralee's fantasy comes next. She is the Lone Ranger—and the boss!—and Hart is her secretary, whom she sexually harasses.

In Violet's dreamworld, she is Snow White, surrounded by Walt Disney cartoon characters. In contrast to her image of purity, she poisons Hart's coffee, just as Snow White's evil stepmother poisoned the apple that Snow White ate. Then all of the female employees, who have been slaves, are freed.

The day after the women fantasize about doing Hart in [killing him], Violet accidentally puts rat poison in his coffee instead of "Skinny and Sweet" sweetener. Although he doesn't actually drink the coffee (in reality he just hits his head and passes out), Violet thinks that she has poisoned him, so she runs to the hospital to explain her mistake. There is a big mix-up and Violet, Judy, and Doralee think that Violet has killed him. Violet then decides to steal Hart's body before the autopsy so that the police won't be able to discover her "crime." They get the wrong body.

The next day, Roz, Mr. Hart's administrative assistant, hears the women discussing the whole story while she is hiding in the ladies' bathroom. As the company "spy," she tells Hart. In attempting to protect themselves from him, reality and fantasy are combined when each of the women's dreams is played out. The three of them take Hart to his house, which is safely empty because Hart's wife has just left for a two-month cruise in the South Seas. They decide that the only way to keep him quiet is to blackmail him. Violet goes through his private files and finds out that Hart has been stealing merchandise and keeping it at the Ajax warehouse, where he later sells it at a high profit.

The women run the office efficiently in their boss's four-to-six week absence—the time it will take the women to prove Hart's dishonest business dealings. While he is away, Judy, Violet, and Doralee change all of the rules: there are flowers on each desk, equal pay for equal work, flexible working hours, day care for the children of all the working women, new paint in lively colors for the walls, lockers, and furniture, job sharing, and employees' alcohol rehabilitation programs, etc. They also get rid of Roz and reinstate Maria Delgado.

The plan works beautifully until Missy, Hart's wife, returns unexpectedly from vacation. Hart gets free and is able to hide his illegal activities. But just before Hart can call the police and have the three women put in jail, the big boss comes down for an inspection. He congratulates Hart for the increase in productivity and rewards him by sending him to Brazil to begin a similar program.

Notes

- The character of Frank Hart is a feminist's nightmare. He is self-absorbed and treats people, especially women, like inferior beings. Women are, first of all, viewed as sex objects. He mentions all of the "ugly" women who work in the office, and he makes daily sexual overtures [advances] to Doralee. When not treated as sex objects, women are merely slaves. Violet and Doralee wait on him, following his every command. A stuffed deer head on Hart's office wall symbolizes his macho image and lack of compassion. His prejudices are made clear by the language he uses: women are "bitches" and "girls." He further belittles women by humiliating them publicly. For instance, when Judy has problems with the copier machine, he raises his voice so that others can hear him yell that any "moron" [stupid person] could operate the machine. Finally, he regularly promotes men and ignores competent women. To him the women's liberation movement is a lot of "crap."

- Violet, complaining of the lower status of women workers and of the fact that they don't get equal pay increases or promotions, calls the office situation a "pink-collar ghetto." In the United States there are "white-collar" workers (administrators, upper management), and "blue-collar" workers (laborers, factory workers, etc.). Pink is the color symbolic of females. What Violet is saying is that women workers don't make enough money, are discriminated against for being female, and have no upward mobility [job advancement]; consequently, many live in poverty.

- The idea for a movie about women workers arose when Jane Fonda was touring the country with her former husband, Tom Hayden, who was running for political office. They interviewed many clerical workers [secretaries] in Boston, Massachusetts, and Cleveland, Ohio (Ansen and Kasindorf 1980, 80).

- Two major criticisms were leveled against *9 to 5*. One was the belief that such superstars as Fonda, Tomlin, and Parton would cause a "thundering roar of clashing egos" (Ansen and Kasindorf 1980, 80). This sexist jibe [insult] is one that is often heard in Hollywood. The assumption is that women always fight among themselves. The second complaint about the film is that it was not "wild or dark enough to qualify it as a truly disturbing farce," yet it was "too silly to succeed as realistic satire" (Ansen 1980, 72–73). It isn't clear why the feminist view in this film was blurred—whether it was fear on the part of financial backers to support an obviously feminist story, or failure on the part of the writer to know how the screenplay would turn out. However, it is obvious that the caricature of Frank Hart has made *9 to 5* "safe" for "everyone to see—including every executive-suite bully in the land" (73).

Themes

- There is the theme of autocracy versus democracy. Men are autocrats—dictators. Women in positions of power don't dictate, they work together. They are supportive of each other and are flexible. They can delegate [assign, give] authority without feeling that their power is threatened.

- The "revolution," that is, the kidnapping of the boss and subsequent "rule" by the women, was not planned. A series of events just opened up the opportunity for the women to take advantage of the situation. Still, the women were not in control; otherwise, Frank Hart would not have received credit from his superior for the work that Judy, Violet, and Doralee had done in his absence. This desire for, but ultimate lack of, female empowerment is a recurrent theme in feminist film.

Previewing Questions
Working Girl

1. How does *Working Girl* show the clash [conflict] between "feminism" and "femininity"? According to the film, which of these emerges victorious [wins]?
2. What are the similarities between *9 to 5* and *Working Girl*? What are the differences?

Working Girl
(1988) dir. Mike Nichols 115 min.
Starring: Melanie Griffith, Sigourney Weaver, Harrison Ford

Setting: New York City

Characters

Tess McGill [Melanie Griffith]—a thirty-year-old secretary in a stock brokerage. She wants a promotion into a management training program, but she hasn't been graduated from an expensive college: her degree was earned after five years at night school.

Katharine Parker [Sigourney Weaver]—Tess's boss. She is a week younger than Tess, but she holds a much higher position in the firm.

Jack Trainer [Harrison Ford]—a high-powered businessman who works in mergers and acquisitions. He is Katharine Parker's (former) boyfriend.

Plot

Tess is a working woman searching for a break, a connection with someone important who can help her get a better job. Because she is tired of the sex maniacs in her office, she moves to another department where her boss is a woman. The boss, Katharine, is just as much a chauvinist [dominant, aggressive person] as the men are in some ways, although she does allow Tess to come to her with new concepts. In fact, Tess is quite happy with her at first.

One day Tess has a good idea that she shares with Katharine: a business, Trask Industries, is interested in buying a television station, but Tess suggests that they buy a radio station first, for several reasons. The best deal is a radio broadcasting company called METRO. Katharine seems receptive to [likes] the idea, but she apparently doesn't do anything about it.

While Katharine is off on a skiing trip, she breaks her leg, so Tess is left in control of the office. During this time, Tess discovers that Katharine has stolen her ideas about Trask Industries. Tess also learns that her boyfriend, Mick, is having an affair with an acquaintance of theirs, Doreen. Tess is now feeling vengeful [wants revenge]. As a result, she appoints herself the "representative" for Katharine Parker. Giving herself this new power, she makes contacts and mixes with other business people who can help her get to the top. At one business party that she attends in Katharine's place, she meets Jack Trainer, with whom she will have a meeting the following day. Jack doesn't identify himself, so she doesn't realize that she has been having drinks (and getting drunk) with someone whom she will have to encounter on a professional basis. Their friendship develops from this point, and at the same time their business dealings with Trask Industries also begin to progress.

The difficulty arises when the charade [the game of appearances that Tess has been playing] is found out. Soon her real identity is made clear, and it seems that her career is over. However, she has the chance to persuade Mr. Trask that the ideas for the company were hers. Convinced, Trask offers her a management position in his company. She and Jack declare their love and everyone lives happily ever after, especially Tess, who is an understanding, fair, and compassionate boss.

Notes

- *Working Girl*, in some respects, is reminiscent [reminds one] of the romantic comedies in which the heroine "must conquer class prejudice with wit, charm, bravado [flair], and a little larceny [theft] before she can win the nice guy" (Corliss 1988b, 78). Though of a lower social class than Katharine, and though not a graduate of a prestigious [having a high reputation] university, Tess manages not only to survive, but also to garner [win] both career and husband. There is a decidedly happy ending: it is the old rags-to-riches story with Cinderella undertones.

- Perhaps part of the appeal of Tess McGill is her femininity. "Here is a woman who dresses like a woman and not like a woman dressed like she thinks a man would dress if he were a woman" (Corliss 1988b, 78).

- *Working Girl* is similar to and different from *9 to 5*, another film about women trying to make it in the workplace, in the following ways:

  —In both films, the boss is suddenly incapacitated and the "lowly" [unskilled, or undereducated, or unappreciated] workers must take over. The women find that they cannot fight the male-dominated system. As far as *9 to 5* is concerned, the female characters work together but achieve only limited success. *Working Girl*, on the other hand, shows two women competing against each other. The one that is perceived to be more feminine is the one that gets the job and the man.

  —Katharine Parker (*Working Girl*) wields [has] power because she is in charge, but she nonetheless feels the ticking of her biological clock. This can be interpreted as meaning that women are incomplete if they don't have a man and children. In contrast, Judy, Violet, and

Doralee of *9 to 5* are liberating themselves from men.
—The tone of *9 to 5* is more optimistic than that of *Working Girl*. In the case of the former, the women work democratically and cooperatively; in the case of the latter, however, women, like men, are capable of using people in order to meet their own personal needs, particularly if they have assumed masculine qualities, as Katharine has.

Theme

- The basic theme of the film can be found in the opening scenes and in the music played during the opening credits. We see the Statue of Liberty and hear the song, "The New Jerusalem," which reflects the theme, promising liberation and upward mobility for the working class, especially for those who are women. The ferry brings the workers into Manhattan every day, just as ships brought foreigners in the old days to the "land of opportunity."

Previewing Questions
Thelma and Louise

1. In what ways is *Thelma and Louise* an optimistic film? In what ways is it pessimistic?
2. What does *Thelma and Louise* seem to be saying about women and the feminist movement?
3. Is the ending of the film believable? If so, why? If not, why not?

Thelma and Louise

(1991) dir. Ridley Scott 130 min.
Starring: Geena Davis, Susan Sarandon

Setting: The story begins in Arkansas and concludes on the road, in the desert Southwest.

Characters

Thelma [Geena Davis]—a naive, trusting, and impressionable [easily influenced by others], housewife, who was married at the age of eighteen to Darryl. She is verbally abused by her husband, who also doesn't allow her to come and go as she pleases. Because she never gets out of the house, she is ready to do anything and to have fun. Any man that flatters her is attractive to her.

Louise [Susan Sarandon]—a clean, tidy, tough-minded, aggressive, and independent waitress. She seems to have a deep resentment and distrust of men.

Darryl [Christopher McDonald]—Thelma's husband, a regional manager of a car dealership. He is an inconsiderate, vain, self-centered man who uses Thelma and expects her to be his slave.

Jimmy [Michael Madsen]—Louise's boyfriend, a musician. He seems to love Louise, but she can't allow herself to really love and trust him.

Hal [Harvey Keitel]—the policeman involved in the murder investigation. He is actually sympathetic to the two women because he realizes that they are victims of circumstance.

Plot

Thelma and Louise decide to go to the mountains for a vacation. Because Thelma is afraid of "psycho killers [madmen] and bears," she takes the gun that Darryl gave her, even though she doesn't know how to use it and refuses to touch it.

On the way they stop at a country-western bar for a few drinks. Thelma gets sick, so her dance partner, Harlan, takes her outside to the parking lot for some fresh air. He tries to rape her. Louise pulls the gun on [aims at] Harlan to protect her friend. When he makes obscene remarks about what he should have done to Thelma, Louise becomes enraged and, without thinking, shoots him dead. Afterward Thelma wants to tell the police, but Louise argues that everyone in the bar saw Thelma dancing and flirting with the man. She feels that everyone, police included, would think that Thelma "was asking for it." Louise tells Thelma that women just don't live in that kind of world, meaning that a woman's word about rape isn't taken seriously.

Both Thelma and Louise are in shock. They keep on driving. Louise's plan is to pick up the $6,700 that her boyfriend, Jimmy, has promised to send to Oklahoma, and then to drive over the border to Mexico, in order to escape U.S. law.

They arrive in Oklahoma City. The money is waiting for them, and so is the uninvited Jimmy. Afraid that Louise is going to leave him, Jimmy gives her an engagement ring. Although she loves him, she doesn't want him to marry her for the wrong reason. Louise feels that it is too late for them anyway: she is a criminal with no future.

At the same time that Louise is occupied with Jimmy, Thelma is in the motel room having wild sex with J. D., a handsome young hitchhiker they had picked up along the road. He later steals the $6,700. Because they are penniless, Thelma robs a convenience store. There is no turning back. For the first time, they have a feeling of power, and, even though they are now wanted by law enforcement in several states, they feel more in control of their lives.

While the two women are driving through the desert, the truth comes out as to why Louise has refused to get to Mexico by way of Texas: sometime in her past she was raped there. This explains why Louise killed Harlan so quickly and easily, and why she distrusts men.

The police eventually catch up with them, and the real chase begins. Thelma and Louise get away temporarily, but they know that the end is near. Although Hal, the police officer assigned to their case, is sympathetic and tries to convince them that they will come to no harm if they surrender, the women refuse to be caught and taken to jail. Instead, Thelma and Louise decide to commit suicide together by driving off a cliff into the Grand Canyon.

Notes

- There are several instances of irony in the film. Here are only two:

    —Thelma packed the gun, even though she was afraid of it and didn't want to use it.
    —Although the women became "wanted criminals," they felt more free and more empowered than at any point in their lives.

- Hats emerge as powerful symbols. The cowboy hat represents the rugged [tough] outlaws that the women have become. (Note that J. D. has a jail record and sports [wears] a cowboy hat.) The baseball cap that the two women steal from the trucker after they blow up his rig [truck] is symbolic of their newly discovered "male" power. (Note further that the baseball hat flies off when the police helicopter appears.)

- The male characters in *Thelma and Louise* are an interesting study:

    —Harlan takes violent advantage of Thelma's weaknesses.
    —Darryl is the stereotypical "male, chauvinist pig" and represents everything vile [nasty] about traditional masculinity.
    —Jimmy has a good heart, but he symbolizes the modern man that is afraid of emotional commitment.
    —J. D. is charming, but he is also completely untrustworthy. His character is vital to the plot development; without him, Thelma would never have learned the fine art of robbing convenience stores. In fact, if he hadn't taken their money, the women would not have been forced to turn to robbery.
    —Hal is a kindly cop. Unfortunately the two women never have a chance to see him as anything but another man who wants to hurt them.

- Though it has been heralded [praised] as a landmark [important] female "buddy [close friend] movie," *Thelma and Louise* has also been criticized as a film that provides poor role models for females, especially young girls. Callie Khouri, the author of the screenplay, argues, however, that Hollywood operates under a double standard: men may appear in action pictures in which violence is considered a healthy fantasy. But when women do the same thing, it is seen as propaganda (Schickel 1991, 55). Khouri's desire was to see what would happen when two women were forced by outside circumstances into becoming fugitives from the law. Would they behave in the same way as men would? *Thelma and Louise* shows the answer to be, "Yes." The basic difference is that the leading female characters have no option but to die at the end of the film.

- It is interesting to note that the popular "women's" movies that have cashed in on [taken advantage of] the success of *Thelma and Louise* have shown women beating up on women, rather than women bonding with women. The following films exemplify this negativism and all were released in 1992: *The Hand that Rocks the Cradle, Single White Female,* and *Death Becomes Her.*

- *Thelma and Louise* is a positive film in that the two women took charge of their own lives, and negative in that their only real freedom came through death. Their suicide is, however, far from being triumphant: "When death is your only choice, how free are you?" (Schickel 1991, 56).

Themes

- *Thelma and Louise* is a story about friendship and females bonding together in encouragement and support.

- Woman as victim: in all of the feminist films described in this chapter—*Pat and Mike, 9 to 5, Working Girl,* and *Thelma and Louise*—women are largely the victims of circumstance. They are placed in bad situations and then try as best they can to overcome their circumstances. Success seems to be directly related to how closely the women fit social expectations of gender roles, i.e., how males and females are supposed to behave. If "feminine," as is Tess (*Working Girl*), or if needful of a man or his advice, as is Pat (*Pat and Mike*), the character is rewarded. If, on the other hand, the female leads are aggressive (*9 to 5*) or violent (*Thelma and Louise*), they are punished.

- This film raises the question of rape and women's rights. Louise killed Harlan because he was attempting to rape her friend, and because she herself was once sexually attacked. Since Thelma was dancing with Harlan, the thinking is that she was "asking for it." Although rape is a crime of violence and not sexual passion, Louise believed, with a fair amount of certainty, that no court would let her go free for her crime.

Chapter 4
Discrimination in Film

Discrimination is not always a pejorative [negative] word. Sometimes it means the act of distinguishing [noticing] differences in quality. To have discriminating taste is good; it suggests the ability to see the difference between superior and inferior things.

However, in recent decades especially, *discrimination* is most often used to mean the unfair treatment of people based not on individual merit [worth] but on group membership. In other words, *to discriminate* has come to mean "to discriminate against." The groups discriminated against may be racial, cultural, religious, class, or gender. And the form of discrimination may range from denying equal educational, professional, or economic opportunities to persecution [harassment], slavery, or even death. In none of its forms is discrimination against people good or admirable.

Discrimination is often used with the words *prejudice* and *bias*, and although they are related, there is an important difference that should be noted. *Prejudice* and *bias* are *beliefs*, expectations of people, based on generalized and uninformed ideas about the groups to which those people belong. *Discrimination*, on the other hand, is *behavior* toward people. Indeed, prejudice and bias often lead to discrimination, but they are not the same.

The most obvious form of discrimination, perhaps, is racial. After all, racial differences such as skin color, facial features, and body and hair type are the easiest to see. Given the tendency of prejudiced discriminators to think in generalities, it is not surprising that they easily find significance in the obvious, though superficial, features of other human beings. Lazy thinking is easy thinking. There are many examples of racial discrimination. The mistreatment of European whites against people of color around the globe is well known, whether it takes place in the United States against Native Americans and blacks or in South Africa, India, and Australia against the indigenous peoples of those countries. There are, however, examples of more subtle [not obvious] forms of discrimination based on less obvious racial or cultural differences: the discrimination of the Japanese against the Koreans, for example, or the discrimination of North Africans against their southern neighbors. Sometimes the discrimination is based on minor racial, cultural, or linguistic differences. Demonstrating very short memories, established immigrant groups in the United States have often met newer immigrant groups with hostility.

Discrimination has for centuries also been grounded in [based on] religious differences. The Crusades of the Middle Ages, in which Christians tried to take Jerusalem from the Muslims, are among the bloodier examples. Furthermore, the blood of holy wars continues to spill into our own time in such diverse places as Bosnia, the Middle East, and India. Perhaps no example of religious discrimination is more extreme, nor more vividly burned into our minds than the extermination [murder] of six million Jews by the Nazis in what we now call the Holocaust. Of course, the inspiration for that dreadful event came not only from religious differences between Christians and Jews, but from racial differences as well (Aryan versus non-Aryan).

Even in societies of homogeneous [same] race and religion, there is discrimination based on social class. In the past, the classes were based on family lines and professions. In modern societies, they are usually based on wealth. In the United States, we are familiar with upper, middle, and lower class, and for those who like to put a fine point on their prejudices, we subdivide those into upper middle, lower middle, upper upper, lower lower, etc. And while class society can be uncomfortable, even cruel, for its members, a caste society, in which people are born into a social group with no chance of escape, is worse.

Among the most hotly debated discrimination issues today are those related to gender and sexuality. For hundreds of years the sexes were considered by most people to be so different that a comparison of their respective civil rights was apparently all but inconceivable [unthinkable]. In most societies and in most times, the role of women seemed so clearly unrelated to that of men and so clearly ordained by either God or Nature that discussions of equality were rare. Then, about a hundred years ago, in England and the United States particularly, women's movements were born in order to secure the right to vote and to have decent working conditions for women. Once those goals were attained, or at least brought within reach, other objectives were defined. Still, many forms of discrimination exist today, and the equal rights amendment, for which women have been working since the early years of the twentieth century, has yet to be ratified [approved]. Apparently, large numbers of both men and women remain blind to this most widespread form of discrimination.

Related to sex (anatomically [structurally] male versus anatomically female) discrimination is discrimination based on sexual preference. The political movement to guarantee equal rights for gays and lesbians really only began after 1969 when a raid [attack] on the Stonewall Bar in Greenwich Village led to riots in protest of police abuse. Moreover, homosexuality and bisexuality are still considered by most people either immoral or pathological [diseased], and the law in many places makes them illegal, so the prejudicial base for discrimination against gays and lesbians is strong.

However, even if all the world were of the same race, the same sex, the same language background, the same religion, and so on, human beings would probably still find differences among themselves that would allow prejudice and discrimination to grow. In the United States, we are confronted by discrimination in a thousand ways: discrimination against old people, against physically challenged [handicapped] people, against people with different accents. Where there is no logical basis for discrimination, we humans have been incredibly clever (or stupid) in finding one. The ability to discern [distinguish] differences is an important skill. Our species would not have survived without it. We wouldn't be able to differentiate between the mushrooms that delight our senses and the ones that stop our hearts. We wouldn't be able to recognize patterns of foliage [plant leaves], cycles of weather, or our own young. It is unfortunate that this valuable survival skill, when applied to our co-inhabitants on earth, is so often abused.

The relationship of film to discrimination is complex. Some films are clearly intended to fight discrimination; others either knowingly or unknowingly reinforce [strengthen] it. There are even some that intend to combat discrimination but inadvertently [accidentally] support it. Perhaps believing that prejudice comes from fear, filmmakers have tried to make the victims of discrimination less fearful and more sympathetic to their oppressors and in so doing have sometimes made them at best pitiable [causing feelings of sympathy], at worst contemptible [causing feelings of disrespect].

Films addressing racial discrimination are numerous. Dealing with black-white relations are such films as *Pinky* (1949), *Imitation of Life* (1959), *A Raisin in the Sun* (1961), *Guess Who's Coming to Dinner* (1967), *Sounder* (1972), *The Autobiography of Miss Jane Pittman* (1974), *Roots* (1977), *The Color Purple* (1985), *Native Son* (1986), *Mississippi Burning* (1988), and *Jungle Fever* (1991). Otherwise prestigious films like *Birth of a Nation*

(1915) and *Gone with the Wind* (1939) have reinforced racial stereotypes, presenting blacks as childish, helpless, or stupid. Indeed, the number of movies made before the 1950s that use blacks only as supernumerary [extra] servants and comic relief is countless. There are films that show other forms of racial discrimination as well. *Little Big Man* (1970) and *Dances with Wolves* (1990) depict discrimination by whites against Native Americans. *Come See the Paradise* (1990) shows the extreme discrimination directed at Japanese Americans during World War Two. *Mississippi Masala* (1991) offers an unusual example of interracial conflict, focusing on Indians (from India) and blacks in the southern United States.

Filmmakers have also dealt with the theme of religious discrimination. *Gentlemen's Agreement* (1947), *The Dark at the Top of the Stairs* (1960), *School Ties* (1994), *Sophie's Choice* (1982), and *Schindler's List* (1994)—the last two part of the extensive filmwork dedicated to showing the horrors of the Holocaust—powerfully depict anti-Semitism. Unlike films that cry out against religious discrimination, there are many that only serve to reinforce the religious prejudices inherent in [basic to] society. Whether the many films that depict Middle Easterners as terrorists over the past two decades are inspired by racial, political, or religious fears is hard to determine, but certainly no sympathetic portrayal of Muslims comes to mind. One film, *Not Without My Daughter* (1991), a prime example of a film meant to combat discrimination against women, in doing so reinforces negative perceptions of Muslims.

Not surprisingly, most of the films discussed in the chapter on feminist films could also be included in this chapter on discrimination in that the feminist agenda is primarily concerned with inequality between the sexes. Certainly *9 to 5* (1980) treats discrimination against women in the workplace as does *Norma Rae* (1979). Films that portray discrimination based on sexual preference include *The Boys in the Band* (1970), *Philadelphia* (1993), *Longtime Companion* (1990), and *The Band Played On* (1994). However, *The Boys in the Band*, as well as two earlier films dealing with homosexuality, *Tea and Sympathy* (1956) and *The Children's Hour* (1962), present such a bleak [hopeless] picture of that condition that they arguably do more harm to homosexuals than good. The protagonist of *Boys in the Band* is so neurotic that pity competes with contempt in audience perceptions. In *Tea and Sympathy*, the suspected homosexual is finally exonerated [cleared] of that odious charge and is granted Deborah Kerr's bosom upon which to prove his intact [complete] manhood. The most terrible fate of all is reserved for the suspected lesbian in *The Children's Hour* who punishes herself with suicide.

Discrimination by one class or ethnic group against another is the theme of such diverse films as *Pygmalion* (1938)/*My Fair Lady* (1964), *Of Human Bondage* (1934, 1946, 1964), *Look Back in Anger* (1959, 1980, 1989), *West Side Story* (1961), *Trading Places* (1983), *A Room with a View* (1985), *Down and Out in Beverly Hills* (1986), *Mystic Pizza* (1988), *Pretty Woman* (1990), and *Howard's End* (1992).

If it were necessary to choose the ultimate example of discrimination in film, the best choice would be the Academy Award-winning *Gandhi* (1982), which manages to depict all of the aforementioned types of discrimination except that against sexual preference. This David Lean epic encompasses [includes] the discrimination of whites against blacks in South Africa, of the English against the Indians, the Hindus against the Muslims, the high castes against the low castes, the middle class of England against the peasant class of India, and even the discrimination of Gandhi himself against his wife and all women before he is enlightened to the contrary.

Previewing Questions
Freaks

1. What is your own definition of *freak*?
2. Notice the socializing done among the characters. Who specifically associates with whom, and why?
3. Does the director, Tod Browning, have any real sympathy for these freaks or is he simply exploiting their handicaps to create sensationalism?

Freaks

(1932) dir. Tod Browning 64 min.
Starring: Leila Hyams, Olga Baclanova, Henry Victor, Wallace Ford

Setting: circus sideshow

Characters

Hans and Frieda [Harry and Daisy Earles]—a midget couple engaged to be married.

Madame Tetralini [Rose Dione]—the mother figure to the freaks.

Cleopatra [Olga Baclanova]—the trapeze artist.

Hercules [Henry Victor]—the muscle man. After kicking out Venus, he becomes the boyfriend of Cleopatra.

Venus [Leila Hyams]—the woman with the seal act. She and Hercules have just broken up, and she fears she will never find the "right man" because she is getting too old.

Phroso [Wallace Ford]—the clown. He is a kind, friendly man who helps Venus feel better after the breakup. He mentions an "operation" he had, so we can assume he had some kind of physical problem, but for practical purposes he is "normal," and he acts as a kind of go-between for the freaks. He is their connection to the normal world.

Daisy and Violet [Daisy and Violet Hilton]—Siamese twins. Daisy will marry the stutterer, Roscoe. Violet falls in love with Mr. Rogers.

Roscoe [Roscoe Ates]—the stutterer.

Joseph/Josephina [Josephine Joseph]—the hermaphrodite (half man/half woman).

The pinheads: Elvira and Ginny Lee [Zip and Pip], and Schlitze [Schlitze]—the three bald, childlike girls.

The Living Torso [Randion]—the black man with no arms or legs.

A dwarf [Johnny Eck]—has no legs; walks on his hands.

The armless girl [Frances O'Connor].

The bearded lady, married to the Human Skeleton—they have a baby and there is much celebration among the freaks (Wolf 1989, 89).

Plot

At the beginning of the film there is a long written introduction. It is difficult to understand and written in highly stylized English, but the main ideas are as follows.

Long ago people believed that anything that was not exactly normal was evil and brought bad luck. Any leader of Europe who had physical deformities was said to be the cause of all that country's misfortune [bad luck]. Furthermore, in history, folk tales, and literature there are many stories about misshapen [deformed] creatures who somehow changed the world: Goliath, Frankenstein's monster, Calaban, and Tom Thumb. Among the common people, an abnormal birth was a sad occasion, and the poor child was usually left outside somewhere to die. If the child survived, it was isolated from society and its family was shamed. Therefore, in order to live, the freak had to beg or steal. Occasionally a rich noble would take the freak into his court to entertain guests. The love of beauty is deep and has been a part of Western civilization for centuries; therefore, people have been psychologically conditioned to feel disgusted by the ugly and the deformed. It is a terrible pity that society avoids them because these poor misshapen humans have normal thoughts and emotions. To protect themselves from the cruel world, these people have created their own code of ethics, rules, and values, which are very strict. This story is about their code. (The introduction also mentions the word *teratology*, which is the science or study of monstrosities or abnormal formations in animals or plants.) As the film opens we hear a man advertising the freak show attraction. His words are important foreshadowing [signals of future events]. Basically he warns the public that the freaks are an accident of birth and that we are lucky to be normal. He states that these physically deformed people didn't ask to be born, but now they are here, and they have their own laws. If a person angers one of the freaks, that person angers all of them. They act as a unit to get revenge. This story is about that revenge, and the film continues in flashback, going back in time to tell the story of the freaks' vengeance.

The plot is very straightforward and easy to follow. The setting is a circus and sideshow of freaks. They keep to themselves, having developed their own community, while the circus performers, who are "normal," either ignore the freaks or ridicule [make fun of] them. One of the freaks, the midget Hans, inherits a fortune. When Cleopatra, the trapeze artist, hears of this, she determines to marry him and then kill him, thereby becoming the beneficiary [recipient] of all his money. Cleo does not have trouble getting a marriage proposal from Hans since he is already in love with her. The complications are that Cleopatra is not a freak and that

Hans already has a fiancée, Frieda, another midget who truly loves him. Paying no attention to the warnings of the other freaks, Hans marries Cleopatra. What happens at the marriage party and during the week that follows is a good illustration of what the man said at the film's beginning. The freaks, learning of Cleopatra's deception, determine that they will enact their own code of ethics in revenge.

Notes

- Tod Browning, the director, was born in Kentucky in 1882 and died in 1962. When he was sixteen he decided to run away and become a member of a traveling circus, where he became a contortionist and a clown. Later he worked in the vaudeville theatre as a comedian and then as an actor. By 1915 he was writing screenplays, and by 1917 he had become a director. The most important point in his career as a director came in 1925 with *The Unholy Three*, about three criminals: a transvestite ventriloquist, a dwarf, and a strong man. His preference for the abnormal and the horrible were clearly present in his films. *Freaks* was the strangest and most controversial of his works. His best-known film is *Dracula*, filmed in 1931, starring Bela Lugosi (Katz 1979, 175).

- *Freaks* was such a shocking film that it was later cut [made shorter and less graphic] and finally taken out of circulation. Its viewing was prohibited in England for thirty years. Only since about the 1970s has it begun to be available to the public again.

- This film is considered a "cult classic" and is also referred to as being "campy." The word *cult* means the veneration [adoration, great respect] of someone or something by a group of admirers. *Camp* concerns the style of the film, which is neither smooth nor natural. Camp is usually meant to be intellectual and amusing.

- There is some limited fraternization [interaction] among the freaks and the regular circus performers. Notice who is on friendly terms with whom.

- One reviewer of this film has stated that director Browning made a big mistake in casting real freaks instead of actors in makeup. For that reason, he argues, the audience cannot distance themselves; they cannot appreciate the art of the film because they are responding to the physical deformities of the freaks (Wolf 1989, 88–89).

- Other notable films that take a sympathetic view of the ugly and the deformed are *The Hunchback of Notre Dame*, *The Elephant Man*, *Frankenstein*, *Phantom of the Opera*, *Mask*, and *Beauty and the Beast*.

Themes

- Like the story itself, one main theme is easy to determine. The golden rule of the Old Testament of the Bible is followed by the freaks: An eye for an eye. Cleo and Hercules tried to kill Hans, so they received what the freaks thought was an equally terrible and violent punishment. On a deeper level, however, the film shows us that the freaks' values are not so simple. Some of the most important scenes of the film are those that show us the everyday routine of the freaks—how they eat, move, and interact. Their values seem to be the true ones, and the normal circus people seem to be the evil ones. The freaks are open-minded, unlike the normal circus performers, and are willing to accept into their circle anyone who is kind to them. We, the audience, may be shocked at the appearance of the freaks, but we have "a warm appreciation for their humanity" (Thomas 1972, 136–37).

- As for the theme of discrimination, it is clear that there is segregation [separation] of the normal circus people from the freaks and that normal human beings, such as Cleo, exploit [use] the abnormal ones for their own profit and amusement. Some critics have even accused director Browning of exploiting the freaks in his film in order to create a sensation and attract an audience.

Previewing Questions
Forbidden

1. How many wars throughout history can you name that have been started because of or have been fueled by religious intolerance?
2. Would you put your life in jeopardy [danger] to save the life of someone whose religion or beliefs were different from your own?
3. Would your life be significantly changed if you were to date or even marry someone outside your own religion?

Forbidden

(1985) dir. Anthony Page   114 min.
Starring: Jacqueline Bisset, Jurgen Prochnow

Setting: Berlin, September 1, 1939, the day Hitler invaded Poland

Characters

Countess Nina von Halder [Jacqueline Bisset]—the narrator of the film, and the main character. She is a German aristocrat of liberal politics and independent ways. After a brief and unfulfilling marriage she has returned to the university to study veterinary medicine. Both of her parents are dead. Her father, of whom she was very fond, died when she was thirteen. Her mother didn't like her very much; in fact, her mother hated many things, including Jews.

Fritz Friedlander [Jurgen Prochnow]—a German Jew. Before the war he published his own magazine, in which he wrote poetry. His father was the first Jewish judge in Germany. He and his mother live in a big fine house that they manage to keep by selling her antiques and jewelry. Although Fritz is a Jew, his first allegiance is to his country, Germany, and particularly to his beloved Berlin. As a child he went to secular rather than to religious schools and thus learned very little about the details of his faith. While other Jews are escaping Germany to save their lives, he refuses, saying that he does not confuse the Nazis with the German people. He believes firmly that the Nazis will disappear, but that the Germans will not.

Plot

The story line follows the development of the relationship between Nina, a Gentile [Christian], and Fritz, a Jew, throughout the course of World War Two, from 1939 to 1945. Nina is first attracted to Fritz when she sees him helping a Jewish store owner defend himself against the Nazis. She appreciates his courage. Later when she meets him formally at the house of her piano teacher, she clearly wants to see him again, even though Christians and Jews are not supposed to mix, as a result of the passage of the Nuremberg Laws. The early plot reveals Nina's transformation into a politically active Jewish sympathizer. The two motivations for her sudden interest in politics are her relationship with Fritz and the arrest for "subversive [politically destructive] activity" of her piano teacher. She finds that most Germans don't care about the Jews. For instance, when she asks a minister if she can help, he tells her that the Church is not really helping the Jews because the clergy [ministers] are afraid for their own future and because most churchgoers hate Jews. Finally Nina gets in touch with the Swedish clergy and begins helping with the underground movement to transport Jews out of Germany. The remainder of the film concerns the difficulties of her continuing, secret relationship with Fritz as they try to survive the war years together without being found out.

Notes

- The Nuremberg Laws were rules set by Hitler that prohibited Jews from having regular jobs or owning their own businesses and that strictly banned intermarriage, or sex, between Jews and Aryans, the master race.

- By 1940 the Jews are being rounded up like cattle. Some, including Fritz, are made to do forced labor, and others are sent to concentration camps.

- By 1943 deportation has reduced Berlin's population of Jews to one-eighth of the original number, or about 20,000. Hitler decides to send away these remaining ones as a part of "The Final Solution" (the wholesale extermination of mass numbers of Jews and other "undesirables"). Nina, meanwhile, works desperately to help these Jews escape.

- The bombings of the city become much worse from 1943 to 1945. Berlin is destroyed. Families and homes are torn apart. This fact is illustrated through the character of Lucy, a little orphan girl whom Nina brings home to live with her and Fritz. Then the Gestapo [the German secret police] break into Nina's home, looking for hidden Jews. (The Nazis were ruthless [without compassion, cruel] in hunting down the Jews, and their spy system was complex and comprehensive [complete].) Even so, Fritz manages to avoid detection.

- In April 1945 the Russians march into Berlin. They find Nina and Fritz, whom they think are "fascisti" [Nazi fascists]. As they prepare to shoot Fritz, he begins to sing a Jewish song. One Russian recognizes the song and Fritz's religion, and his life is spared [saved]. Ironically Fritz is saved by his religion, which has cost him six years of hardship and exile.

- Fritz's friend Max is good for Fritz in two ways: first, he keeps Fritz from being lonely, and second, he is able to give Fritz a better understanding and a clearer appreciation of his religious heritage by teaching him old Jewish songs and scripture passages.

- News of Nina's pregnancy is well received by Fritz and his mother. The point seems to be that the Jews respect and rejoice in life while the Nazis and the Gestapo, on the other hand, are working to destroy the lives of millions of people.

- The homosexuals of Germany, as represented by Nina's friend, are treated as inferior and aberrant [abnormal], just as the Jews are. Hitler's plan was to create a master race of Nordic Aryans, a superior, creative people who would dominate the world. Any group or race of people who deviated from the model were to be eliminated [killed] in order to keep the master race pure. In his book *Mein Kampf*, he spoke strongly against miscegenation [the mixing of the races]. Above all, he preached against international Jewry [the domination of the world economy, religion, and politics by the Jews]. Many Germans actually believed in their racial superiority as Aryans. Groups that were targeted for elimination included the Jews, homosexuals, and blacks.

Themes

- The main characters of this film are both German. This is not a film that asks its viewers to hate and blame all Germans. Fritz's undying faith in his fellow Germans, echoed in these words, is important to the film's message: "I try not to confuse the Nazis with the German people."

- Clearly the point of the film is to show the suffering of the Jews as a result of Nazi persecution. However, unlike more graphic and violent depictions of the Jewish condition, such as the film *Schindler's List* and the two TV series *The Winds of War* and *War and Remembrance*, this made-for-television movie views the war and the victimization of the Jews from a personal perspective by involving the audience with only two main characters rather than with a family or a large segment of the population.

Previewing Questions
The Accused

1. Who is "the accused"?
2. Should witnesses to a rape be held responsible in some legal way if they don't try to help the victim?

The Accused

(1988) dir. Jonathan Kaplan   110 min.
Starring: Jodie Foster, Kelly McGillis

Setting: a large U.S. city

Characters

Sarah Tobias [Jodie Foster]—the rape victim. A lower-middle-class waitress whose hobby is making astrology charts for her friends. She lives in a trailer (her own) with a drug-dealing, motorcycle-riding musician named Larry. For fun she parties with her friends, smoking pot [marijuana] and drinking too much.

Katherine Murphy [Kelly McGillis]—a lawyer for a large, impersonal law firm. She is also the deputy district attorney.

Plot

One night while out with her girlfriend Sally at a local bar called The Mill, and while very drunk and stoned [on drugs], Sarah is thrown upon a pinball machine and raped by three men. Escaping into the street she hitches [gets] a ride with a truckdriver to the hospital, where tests are run to confirm the physical evidence necessary to make formal rape charges. The staff members there ask her many questions, as if they don't believe her story. They are very cold and impersonal to her.

After Katherine becomes Sarah's attorney, she interviews her client and finds that Sarah's character is questionable [of doubtful respectability]. If the rape case goes to trial, Katherine fears that Sarah will lose because:

(a) Sarah had been drunk and stoned that night.
(b) Sarah had told her friend that she would like to "screw" [have sex with] one of the men there who later raped her.
(c) Sarah is a common waitress who lives with a man to whom she is not married.
(d) Sarah has a criminal record of drug possession.
(e) There are no witnesses—or none who will volunteer.

Believing she can't win, Katherine goes to the lawyers of the three rapists and cuts a deal [makes a bargain]. Katherine accepts "Reckless Endangerment" as the charge. This is still a felony [a very serious crime]. When Sarah finds out, she is enraged because the rapists aren't punished for the crime of rape. Her violation by them is ignored. In fact, before the deal, one lawyer for the three men tells a TV interviewer that there was no rape. He claims that Sarah, the "so-called victim," was enthusiastic about having sex with the three men. He further informs the interviewer that she put on a sex show.

The turning point for Katherine, when she begins to develop sympathy for Sarah and to have the desire to help Sarah have the opportunity to speak out for herself in court, is when (a) Sarah tells her that she thinks of herself as trash and (b) the tattooed man tells Katherine he enjoyed watching Sarah's sex show. Katherine's law firm is against her reopening the case. She gets no support from her colleagues, but her argument is that she owes Sarah. For the sake of justice, and for Sarah, Katherine jeopardizes [risks] her job.

Because in the U.S. judicial system a person or persons cannot be tried again for the same crime, Katherine decides to prosecute the witnesses on charges of criminal solicitation instead. Thus Sarah finally has her day in court, and the testimony of her rape is heard. Largely because of the testimony of Kenneth Joyce, a college frat [fraternity] boy whose buddy raped Sarah that night, justice is served.

Notes

- This film was based loosely on an actual trial in which the assailants [attackers] were acquitted [found not guilty].

- Sarah's character presents a stark contrast to that of Katherine. Sarah is the product of a broken home, her father having left her mother before Sarah was born. Her mother lives elsewhere, and with a series of men. Her only communication with her mother comes when Sarah is in trouble or needs money. Familial love is clearly absent. Katherine, on the other hand, is well educated, sophisticated, self-confident, and articulate [fluent]. Whereas Sarah deals with emotions and astrological signs in her interactions with people, Katherine is reserved, analytical and, apparently, not very warm and compassionate. By story's end, however, each woman has acquired some of the better qualities of the other. Sarah has developed a kind of dignity and self-respect, and Katherine has learned how to be more sympathetic and openly caring.

- Even though Sarah pretends to be very tough, the trauma and horror of the rape eventually begin to bother her. She changes her look by cutting her hair short and by kicking her boyfriend Larry out of her house because he is unsupportive. The culmination [highest point] of her frustration and anger at being in this unjust situation comes when she rams her car into the truck of one of the witnesses to her rape. She later tells Katherine at the hospital that the witness thinks of her as "a piece of shit." Therefore she believes that everybody thinks of her as trash. Her self-image suffers.

- Because of the way the judicial system is set up, the victim of rape is, in reality, the one who is on trial. She is considered guilty of having provoked the rape until she can prove that she didn't "ask for it." The rape victim is the accused, just as the alleged assailant is also the accused. This is clear from the questions that are asked of rape victims: Do you have a criminal record? What were you wearing that night? Have you ever made love to more than one man at a time? Have you ever been hit by a man? If so, did you enjoy it? Do you smoke pot and drink often? Do you go to bars alone a lot? Do you wear underwear when you go to those bars? Have you ever had an abortion?

- The title of the film thus has a double meaning. In this society, a woman who has been raped is blamed, or accused, almost to the same extent as the rapist (Kauffmann 1988, 31). This culture has a bad habit of blaming the victim. "We blame the poor for poverty. We blame the homeless for being in the street" (Corliss 1988a, 127). We blame women when they are attacked, as if the woman were at fault for what happened.

- Katherine's prosecution of the witnesses on the grounds of criminal solicitation is a groundbreaking precedent [the first case of its kind]. No one has ever before tried to prosecute witnesses to a rape. By definition criminal solicitation states that if a person induces, encourages, commands, or entreats another person to commit a felony, then she or he is guilty.

- "Rape 1" is the strongest penalty for rape and carries a maximum sentence of twenty years. Mike Tyson, the famous U.S. boxer, was imprisoned on this charge. Lesser but still serious offenses are "Sexual Abuse 2" or "Rape 2," which include a prison term of two to five years with most men getting out after only eight or nine months. All of these crimes are clearly sexual offenses. Most sex offenders, interestingly, get out of jail after serving only one year. The lawyers defending the three men who attacked Sarah make a deal for their clients to be charged with "Reckless Endangerment" because that plea doesn't have the sexual implications that might hurt the men's reputations.

- The importance of the outcome of Sarah's trial: (a) Sarah gets the satisfaction of telling in court the story of her rape experience; (b) the three rapists, already in jail, will spend all five years in jail instead of a few months; (c) the charge of "Rape" goes on record rather than just the "Reckless Endangerment" charge; and (d) for the first time in history, spectators of a rape, not just the rapists themselves, are held responsible for the rape for having encouraged it.

- Statistics indicate that in cases in which there is more than one attacker, no one tries to help the victim. In other words, if a woman is assaulted [attacked] by two or more rapists, people don't want to get involved or take the responsibility for helping her (Corliss 1988a, 127).

- Data suggest that one woman out of every twelve will be the victim of rape or attempted rape during her lifetime. Rape experts believe the number of victims is even higher than that because women don't always report a rape, especially if the rapist was an acquaintance. If acquaintance rape is included in the statistics, the number of women raped is approximately one in four (Jasper 1992, 80–81).

- Kelly McGillis, the actress who plays Sarah's lawyer, has special insight into the issue of rape, having herself been raped.

Themes

- Rape is not a crime of passion. It is a violent crime. The victim's background is not relevant. "Sexy talk and [sexy] dress in a woman do not equal a permit for sexual attack" (Kauffmann 1988, 31).

- One producer of the film had clear objectives about what she and her coproducer hoped this picture would accomplish: "We're hoping that no one seeing *The Accused* will ever again believe that rape is sexy or that any woman asks for it." A screenwriter for the movie, Tom Topor, also had admirable goals for writing it: "We were saying [to the audience], 'As a spectator you're part of the problem. What would you have done?'" (Corliss 1988a, 127).

Previewing Questions
Do The Right Thing

1. Director Spike Lee suggests that in order to deal with racial (black/white) tensions and to equalize rights and freedoms, we must choose one of two alternatives: a nonviolent approach or a violent attack by the oppressed [the black segment] on the white authority. Note the title. What <u>is</u> the right thing to do according to this film?
2. Many characters in this movie are stereotypes rather than well-developed personalities. Do you recognize them? What is the point of having such stereotypical characters?

Do The Right Thing
(1989) dir. Spike Lee 120 min.
Starring: Spike Lee, Danny Aiello

Setting: a block in Bedford-Stuyvesant, Brooklyn, New York, the hottest day of the summer

Characters

Mookie [Spike Lee]—a pizza delivery person. Not a very responsible or motivated worker, his main concern is getting paid. He has a Chicana girlfriend, Tina [Rosie Perez]. They have a son, Hector, but Mookie doesn't really care about either of them. He only visits when he wants to do "the nasty" [have sex].

Sal [Danny Aiello]—the owner of the pizzeria. A white man in a black neighborhood, he has two deeply prejudiced sons, Vito and Pino [John Turturro]. He has been in business at that location for twenty-five years. Unlike his sons, Sal enjoys the blacks who come to his restaurant, pointing out to his sons that those people put money in his pocket. He says he's proud to have watched the young people grow up on his food.

Jade [Joie Lee]—Mookie's sister. She serves as the conscience of her brother and is the symbolic value system of the neighborhood. Her goal is to do something positive for her community. Her advice to Mookie is to take care of his responsibilities and to go to work.

Mother Sister [Ruby Dee]—another largely symbolic character. Her name is illustrative of the confusion of social roles. She is both mother and sister to her community. She assures everyone that she is always watching over them, and she believes that all the blacks are brothers and sisters, united in their skin color and social situation.

Da Mayor [Ossie Davis]—an elderly, soft-spoken drunk who fancies himself "The Man" [the white man, or a person of political or financial power]. The mayor wears a white suit as if he were in a position of authority. He makes a bit of money by doing odd jobs for Sal. His are the values of an earlier age. From his advice, "Do the right thing," comes the title. He hates no one and believes everyone should live and work together peacefully.

The triumvirate [group of three] consists of Sweet Dick Willie [Robin Harris], M. L. [Paul Benjamin], and Coconut Sid [Frankie Faison]. They don't take an active part in the plot, but they are an important part of the framing of the story. Like the Greek chorus of ancient plays, they watch the actions around them and make appropriate commentary (Glicksman 1989, 13). They reflect the various views of the community when they try to make sense of the world around them. For example, they can't figure out how the Koreans can come into their neighborhood and, in less than a year, be financially successful, whereas black people don't seem to be able to achieve success. One of them remarks that either the Koreans are geniuses or the blacks are stupid. Another one says it's a clear case of discrimination: Black people can't make a success because of their color. The other says he's tired of hearing that same old excuse.

Mr. Señor Love Daddy [Sam Jackson]—the disk jockey (DJ) and amateur philosopher of the neighborhood. From his living room window he watches and reports on the action in the community while playing black music. He seems to take the position of Martin Luther King, Jr. At the end of the film he asks the listeners if they are going to learn to live together. He tells them that they must be more aware, that they should register to vote, and that they should "chill" [be calm].

Radio Raheem [Bill Nunn]—a big, muscular man with a giant portable stereo. He plays only one song: "Fight the Power," by the group Public Enemy. The main idea of this rap song is for African Americans to fight the white authority in order to get equal rights and freedom. Raheem is always alone and is generally respected (or feared) because of his size. He wears brass knuckles with the words *love* and *hate* printed on them. He tells Mookie the story of the world, saying that it is simply about the never-ending struggle between love and hate. What happens to him is what sparks the violence later in the film.

Bugging Out [Giancarlo Esposito]—the Malcolm X representative. He wants to stir up anger and hatred, to bring about change for the neighborhood by making everyone more aware of the injustice of the situation of blacks in the slums. He tells Mookie to stay black—to keep his own values and identity as a black American—rather than try to play the game of the white people.

Smiley [Roger Smith]—a stuttering man with cerebral palsy [a disease of the brain affecting the muscles] who wanders through the film selling copies of a picture of Martin Luther King, Jr., and Malcolm X. His presence is vital. Director Spike Lee is asking the audience to choose their philosophy: the doctrine of nonviolence espoused [supported] by King or the violence of Malcolm X. The fact that Smiley has a speech impediment [problem] is symbolic of his (and others') inability to articulate [speak] his choice.

Plot

The opening scene is of a female dancing to rap rhythms in a series of moves that are similar to boxing steps and boxing punches. In fact, late in the dance, she is actually wearing boxing gloves. The words of the song she is dancing to, and the song Radio Raheem will play again and again, contain the following lyrics: "Fight the power. We got to fight the powers that be. . . . Elvis don't mean nothin' to me. . . . Most of my heroes don't appear on no stamp . . ." (Glicksman 1989, 12). This sets the stage for the violence to come.

The plot itself is simple and the interactions of the characters carry the story. Basically the film follows the everyday lives and troubles of an inner-city neighborhood. The social focal point of the area is Sal's pizza place. Everyone seems to be coexisting peacefully until Bugging Out makes a scene at the pizzeria. Tensions rise as he asks Sal why there are only pictures of white, Italian Americans like Frank Sinatra, Al Pacino, and Robert De Niro on his "Hall of Fame" wall. Bugging Out insists that because the pizzeria clientele are black the wall should contain pictures of black heroes. A small argument starts and Bugging Out decides to boycott Sal's place. Time passes and passions—and the temperature—rise. Eventually Bugging Out starts a big fight that results in Sal's losing his temper and crushing Radio Raheem's jam box while calling the two "niggers." A fight starts. The police arrive and "accidentally" kill Radio. Mookie then throws a garbage can through the window of the pizzeria and the chaos and destruction begin. Sal's place is destroyed.

Notes

- The incident between Radio Raheem and the police was, ironically, a foreshadowing of what happened in the racially motivated Los Angeles riots of 1992. Even at the time this film was released in 1989, New York City was in the middle of a racial problem. A white woman had just been gang raped and beaten by a group of young African Americans in Central Park. Spike Lee points out that two days later a black woman was found raped and murdered in that same park, but the newspapers didn't make a big story of it. Lee states, "That's a devaluation of a black life. It's like black life doesn't mean anything, doesn't count for anything" (Glicksman 1989, 12–15).

- The heat is miserable and is an important ingredient in the violence that erupts. The discomfort that everyone suffers as a result of the heat is mentioned again and again. The air conditioner in the pizzeria is not working. The slums don't have air conditioning. The only temporary relief comes when some boys open the fire hydrant up and the young people go out to play in the cool water.

- Lee chose to film *Do The Right Thing* in the Brooklyn ghetto because he has a deep love for the common African American and the inner-city "street-corner society" (Klawans 1989, 98). In fact, he filmed the movie in the actual slums of Bedford-Stuyvesant, or Bed-Stuy. His crew destroyed three crack houses [places where illegal drugs are used and sold] and cleaned up the street, building a pizzeria and painting murals on the walls of some of the buildings. The film is a "black insider's perspective on the contradictions and celebrations of African-American life" (Glicksman 1989, 12–13).

- The structure of this film is set up in episodes. There are short, dramatic moments between characters, and the action builds as the heat builds. Two characters help to structure and interpret the action. One is Mister Señor Love Daddy and the other is Da Mayor. The three unemployed older men also help judge the action and characters by adding their own interpretations (Klawans 1989, 99).

- There was a time in early Hollywood history that black people couldn't appear in films with white actors. When, on occasion, they did appear, they only sang, danced, or worked as servants: their parts were not important to the film. The reason for this was that audiences in some areas of the country, like the South, didn't want to see blacks in movies, so their parts were cut from the films shown in those regions.

Themes

- Stereotypes are an important thematic part of the film, indicating that the continuation of the ignorance that causes stereotypes is what prevents deeper understanding and better human relations. Some of these stereotypes include the Italian Americans, who are characterized as being loud, prejudiced, ignorant, and family oriented. Another group is the Chicanos, poor Puerto Ricans who keep an unstable peace with the blacks but are unable to make enough money to escape the slums. The blacks are stereotyped, too. The three older men, the mayor, and many other of the block's citizens are not employed. And Mookie represents the young, unmarried, irresponsible black father. The Koreans are typed as hard-working, quiet people who take job possibilities from the blacks. The Italian Americans feel superior to the Chicanos, who feel superior to the blacks, who feel, in certain respects, superior to the Koreans. The young also feel superior to the old: a group of young, disrespectful black people tell the mayor to get a job. They are not interested in his painful life history.

- This film concludes with quotes by two famous black leaders. Director Lee is asking the audience to choose the philosophy of one or the other.

    Martin Luther King, Jr.'s quote is "The old law of an eye for an eye leaves everybody blind" (Glicksman 1989, 13). Clearly he was advocating nonviolent change. King (1929–68) was a charismatic, articulate black Baptist minister who was the leader of the civil rights movement in the United States from the middle of the 1950s until his assassination. In 1964 he received the Nobel Peace Prize for his principles of nonviolent resistance applied to the struggle for racial equality.

    Malcolm X's quote is "I am not against violence in self-defense. I don't even call it violence when it's self-defense, I call it intelligence" (Glicksman 1989, 13). Malcolm X (1925–65) was an assumed name. His father was assassinated for his work with black civil rights. His mother became mentally unbalanced, and Malcolm and his brothers and sisters were put in foster homes. Malcolm X believed that the cause of the blacks' poor social position was "Whitey" [the white man]. He felt that integration wouldn't work, that if civil rights leaders continued to espouse integration, the result would be violence. He argued that the Black Muslim separatists' views were correct and that blacks had to build and maintain their own separate society. In other words, only blacks could empower themselves. Malcolm could foresee a separate society of blacks becoming a separate country in the United States instead of returning to Africa to their roots. He embraced Islam because in that religion there is no color bar. Christianity, he believed, was the white man's religion, and any black that believed in it was slave to Whitey and to Whitey's value system.

Chapter 5
Aspects of the Romantic Comedy

The romantic comedy was probably the most successful style of movie to emerge from the classical age of the American cinema, the era of the 1930s and 1940s. It was later called the "screwball" comedy, probably as a result of Carole Lombard's dizzy [silly] character in *My Man Godfrey* (1936). The year 1934 was the turning point. Movies like *The Thin Man, It Happened One Night, The Gay Divorcée* and actors like Irene Dunne, Carole Lombard, Cary Grant, William Powell, Myrna Loy, and Fred Astaire began the genre (Harvey 1987, xi–xii).

The year 1934, when romantic comedy really became popular, was also the year that the Production Code began to be more strictly enforced. This code was a kind of ethics barometer [measure], to indicate how risqué [shocking] or unacceptable the dialogue and behavior of the actors were. Screen lovers couldn't be as sexy anymore, so they became funny instead. Thus comedies got crazier, and they also got less sexy and more romantic.

The screwball heroine and romantic comedy of the 1930s and 1940s began to fade out after World War Two. Films became more literal, and the behavior of the characters was supposed to be more "grown-up." Silliness was no longer acceptable; acting nice and being sensible were. The new stars were charming and uncomplicated. The new female image was the girl-next-door type. Marriage and traditional family values were very important. Screwball couples who didn't act like the community around them were no longer to be respected and envied for being different.

Characteristics of the Romantic Comedy

- These films exhibit a certain complexity. Human beings are unpredictable, full of surprises, and foolishly inconsistent (Harvey 1987, 15).

- The leading characters are independent, self-assured, and very glamorous (Harvey 1987, 61). The female leads are often particularly glamorous and bright (72).

- The romantic couple can also be terrible: strong willed and bragging [speaking too well of themselves].

- The romantic comedy is usually centered around one thing: the couple themselves—they are intelligent, unpredictable, and entertaining.

- Often in these comedies the male is the weaker sex. Emotional and insecure, he is often out of control and requires large amounts of ego stroking. He is, therefore, the more feminine side of the couple while the female, by contrast, is the strong and solid one. She is powerful and self-possessed [calm] (Harvey 1987, 66).

- Both male and female leads in a romantic comedy often act childish instead of mature (Harvey 1987, 68).

- Often there is a kind of love triangle. There is the "Other Man," who may be tall and big yet doesn't have enough "masculine authority" to be a real challenge. Or there is the "Other Woman," who has no social graces [manners]. When the screwball couple break up, they seem to try to escape their own intelligence and honesty by surrounding themselves with country people or members of the lower class. These others represent the dullness of the world, the everyday boredom, stupidity, and security. But ultimately the screwball couple reject the banal [boring] social norms because they are bright and energetic and are superior to everyday realities. This is often symbolized at the end of the film by the couple's leaving town, leaving sense and sanity behind.

- The romantic comedy usually concerns class and social status. The characters are often rich, cosmopolitan [worldly], and sophisticated, yet the irony is that making such class distinctions is wrong. Most Americans don't respond well to or relate easily to the monied class. Americans prefer to think of themselves as a middle-class, or even as a classless society; thus, making fun of the rich, and having the rich make fun of themselves, is quite a joke (Harvey 1987, 74–75).

- In the romantic comedy, love can't be too melodramatic or emotional, nor can it be too cold and ridiculing. Love should be dignified, practical, and respectful. This is what its characters must discover during the course of the film (Harvey 1987, 81).

- In the original screwball comedies, the comic couples always have some kind of a pet, and by choice, are childless (Harvey 1987, 123).

- The tone of the romantic comedy is skeptical [doubting], and the conversation consists of a lot of short, witty dialogue called one-liners.

- Romantic comedy heroines are often newspaperwomen or independent, aggressively verbal types.

- The setting is often the big city: nightclubs, newspaper offices, luxury apartments. Such settings indicate a certain level of sophistication.

- The lead characters of a screwball comedy make fun of small-town America, characterizing it as boring and full of small, mean, ignorant, rural [country] folk (Harvey 1987, 155–56).

- In romantic comedy the dialogue is always smart and fast. There is lots of playful chatter [talk] between the lead characters. There are many jokes and mischievous [teasing] adventures—and even slapstick [visual humor].

- In this genre the dialogue is especially fast paced, and the audience must listen carefully to catch all the witty dialogue and double entendre.

Previewing Questions
Bachelor Mother

1. Read the section entitled "Aspects of the Romantic Comedy." How does this film fit the genre? How is it different?
2. Consider the social ramifications of being an unmarried mother. How would people view a woman in such a situation in the 1930s? And today?
3. In what ways is the elder Mr. Merlin a very important character?

Bachelor Mother

(1939) dir. Garson Kanin 81 min.
Starring: Ginger Rogers, David Niven

Setting: New York City, Christmastime

Characters

Polly Parrish [Ginger Rogers]—a working girl with no family in the area. She's been temporarily employed for the Christmas business rush at Merlin's department store. She's a very strong, practical girl with no illusions about the real world.

David Merlin [David Niven]—the son of the owner of Merlin's department store. He's a spoiled rich son, having had too many women and too many long nights of partying. He's not very responsible, but he matures after being with Polly and the baby.

John P. Merlin [Charles Coburn]—a strong-willed, crusty [rude], old man who acts more like a dictator than a father. Yet it is because of him, and not his lazy son, that the department store is so successful. He is an imposing, authoritarian figure who is short-tempered and rude, but soft and gentle underneath.

Plot

Polly is a salesgirl in a big department store called Merlin's. One day, while walking around New York City looking for a new job, she sees a woman leave a baby on the doorstep of a home for foundlings [abandoned or orphaned babies]. She goes up to check on the baby, the door opens, and the woman inside immediately assumes that this is Polly's baby. When she denies this, they report her to her store. The store gives her job back to her plus a raise in pay, but she finds that in order to keep her job she has to keep the baby. As if that misunderstanding weren't enough, Freddie Miller, her coworker and dance partner, soon begins to think that Polly is secretly dating the boss's son. No matter what she does or says, no one believes her story about the baby or David. However, she nearly always maintains her composure [stays calm] and accepts what life has to give her, as every good working girl must. Then David's father, old Mr. Merlin, is given an anonymous letter (from Freddie, who's angry about his demotion), which states that David is the father of the baby. When Polly understands that Mr. Merlin knows, she begins to fear that the rich and powerful old man will try to take away the baby, whom she now loves. She doesn't want this to happen, so she pretends to have a father for the baby. The problem is that David also produces a fake father. Old Mr. Merlin isn't fooled, but in the chaos [disorder] that follows, love triumphs [wins].

Notes

- While most of the screwball couples of the 1930s and 1940s era were very cosmopolitan and well-off [rich] financially, many of the single women were working-girl heroines. They were usually practical types who fit well into the everyday work environment, who looked comfortable in their jobs in front of a typewriter or behind a cash register. They were self-assured and sarcastically witty [funny].

- The scene in the club on New Year's Eve is a classic example of the screwball couple's attitude toward phony people and rich snobs. Polly poses as a Swedish girl who speaks no English because she fears speaking to the upper class, with whom she has nothing in common. David makes a lot of sarcastic remarks to indicate his disdain [contempt] and aloofness [indifference]. Then finally they escape the scene and meet in the "real" world and come together in a New Year's Eve celebration kiss that tells the audience that they don't care about the stuffy attitudes of others, they can do what they please.

- Polly has no appropriate evening wear for her date with David, so checking her closet for shoe and clothing size, he calls his department store and orders an outfit sent to her. She's just like Cinderella, going out with her Prince Charming.

- Most screwball couples had an animal rather than a baby. This film appears to be different in that there is a baby. But in fact it isn't different, because this movie does not completely embrace [adopt] the joys of motherhood and family life. What we have is an unwilling and unwed mother. Such a situation hints at sexual scandal and is definitely outside the traditional socially acceptable female role. Given the fact that romantic comedies of the 1930s and 1940s definitely did not believe in the traditional, boring life of everyday people, this film, therefore, does not violate the spirit of the genre by adding the baby but rather reinforces it.

- The slapstick and jokes are played down, understated, more subtle [not obvious]. The movie's style is quietly confident and self-assured, with no need for big displays [demonstrations] of visual humor.

- A character like the elder Mr. Merlin was often to be found in romantic comedies. Such a man is always rich and bossy but has a heart of gold and is always generous with his money to those whom he loves or feels sympathy for. The original "Merlin" was a magician in King Arthur's court, and Old Man Merlin in this film also has a kind of magic—like a fairy godmother. He is, in a sense, smarter than the other characters. It is because of his sanity and wholeness, his consuming desire to have his grandson, that Polly and David can finally be brought together.

Themes

- As is true of classic romantic comedies, *Bachelor Mother* makes fun of traditional values by having as the main character an unwed mother. And the upper class is ridiculed as well. However, unlike other romantic comedies, this movie has a family-oriented ending, a return to those traditional values.

- The couple, Polly and David, along with the baby, come together as a family, and they conform to society rather than running away or leaving town, as most classic romantic comedy couples do. Just as importantly, they represent the marriage of the upper and lower classes. There is harmony and balance.

Previewing Questions
The Thrill of It All

1. Notice the heavy emphasis on the traditional values of home and family. This is a departure from the classic romantic comedy. In what other ways does this film differ dramatically from the original romantic comedy?
2. How does this film ridicule the advertising business?

The Thrill of It All
(1963) dir. Norman Jewison 108 min.
Starring: Doris Day, James Garner

Setting: Early 1960s. Suburbia. New York City.

Characters

Dr. Gerald (Jerry) Boyer [James Garner]—a successful obstetrician [baby doctor]. He delivers babies.

Mrs. Beverly Boyer [Doris Day]—the doctor's wife, a housewife and mother of two.

Maggie—their daughter.

Andy—their son.

Olivia—the first housekeeper.

Mrs. G.—the second housekeeper.

Mr. Frawley (the elder)—owner of the Happy Soap Company and sponsor of the TV series *The Happy Playhouse*.

Mr. and Mrs. Gardner Frawley—a middle-aged couple expecting their first child. Gardner is the son of the elder Frawley and works for him. They are very wealthy.

Plot

The story revolves around the problems of a happily married, upper-middle-class family, the ideal American family. Dr. Boyer and his wife are invited to a dinner party at the Frawleys' to celebrate Mrs. Frawley's pregnancy. Mr. Frawley, the owner of the Happy Soap Company, meets Beverly, whom he thinks is the perfect housewife, and he decides that hers is the image he wants on his TV commercial. She represents home, family, children, domesticity, and all that is good and pure.

Because the public loves Beverly's fresh and sincere approach to making a commercial, she's given a one-year, $80,000 contract. Jerry doesn't want her to work. He prefers that she stay at home and take care of the children. She argues, saying that her current lifestyle is not fulfilling [complete] enough. She claims that she needs outside interests.

She promises that her work won't interfere with her household duties, but she has to spend more and more time posing for advertising photos and making commercials. The house seems to fall apart when she's away. People also begin to recognize her, so she becomes a celebrity [famous].

All of this irritates her husband. Meanwhile we, the audience, are reminded of life's real truth: Mrs. Frawley tells Dr. Boyer, while in his office, that the greatest fulfillment in life is having a baby.

After the company puts in a free swimming pool in Beverly's backyard, Jerry and Bev have a big fight and he walks out on her. Then Jerry has a little talk with a psychiatrist whose office is near his, and he decides he should be more understanding and accommodating. But in fact what Jerry has really decided to do is to try to make his wife jealous.

Meanwhile Mrs. Frawley goes into labor while at a party. Two traffic jams and much confusion later, the baby is born and Beverly comes to the realization that her place is in the home, as a doctor's wife. The implication is that soon she, too, will have another baby.

Notes

- Notice the many domestic scenes at the beginning of the film: an older woman tells her husband she's pregnant; a doctor tells an expectant father that his wife has just had a little girl; this same doctor calls his home and we see his wife taking care of two young children; later we see him kissing his wife in the back seat of a limousine.

- The first commercial we see for Happy Soap, with a sexy young woman in a tub of bubbles, is supposed to be the antithesis [opposite] of all that is domestic and family oriented.

- This film makes fun of the world of advertising, and especially of advertising executives. These men say whatever the boss wants to hear. They don't seem capable of thinking creatively. They make big mistakes, like putting a sexy young girl in a soap commercial when they should realize that housewives, not husbands, will be buying the groceries. Also, the silly playhouse theatre on TV uses exactly the same story each week. The players simply change costumes. The executives think the American public is too stupid to notice this, but, in fact, even the Boyers' young children can see the similarities.

- This film has a few similarities with the romantic comedy of the 1930s and 1940s. There is a lot of slapstick [visual humor]; there are many mistakes made, and many misunderstandings. One example of slapstick humor: the foaming suds in the pool. One example of a misunderstanding: the unsuccessful attempts to communicate with Mrs. G., the German housekeeper.

- Another similarity is that like the romantic comedy of old, the heroine of this film, Beverly, is the strong partner, but only for a while, because unlike the original romantic comedy, in the end the power is transferred back to the previously strong husband when Bev decides to give up her job and be a doctor's wife and a full-time mother.

- Like *Bachelor Mother*, this film embraces the traditional values of home and family.

Themes

- Money talks (as evidenced by the Frawleys) and TV advertising is big business; it influences people.

- Women belong in the home. It's okay for them to have hobbies, such as making home-bottled catsup, but to work outside the home is to invite destruction of the ideal, traditional home setting.

- Having a baby is the most fulfilling part of life for women. The first two themes are very interesting and represent the thinking of the early 1960s. Later in the decade the feminist movement made more progress and women began to reject these simple beliefs, although the original role of women to be housewives and mothers was still strong even into the 1970s.

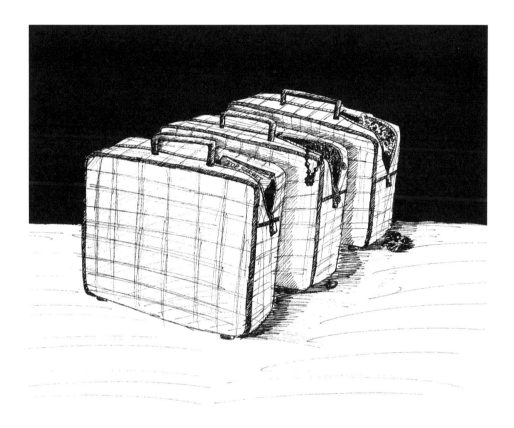

Previewing Questions
What's Up, Doc?

1. What are the similarities and differences between *What's Up, Doc?* and the classic romantic comedy?
2. As is often the case with comedies, there are many stereotypical characters. Which characters can be so identified?

What's Up, Doc?
(1972) dir. Peter Bogdanovich 94 min.
Starring: Barbra Streisand, Ryan O'Neal

Setting: San Francisco, California

Characters

Dr. Howard (Steve) Bannister [Ryan O'Neal]—a musicologist visiting San Francisco (from Iowa) for a conference. He's the stereotypical absent-minded professor type. He is one of the two finalists for a Laraby Foundation grant of $20,000.

Eunice Burns [Madeline Kahn]—Howard's fiancée. She is very boring and acts more like Howard's mother than his girlfriend.

Judy Maxwell [Barbra Streisand]—a university student who tends to cause accidents wherever she goes. A very bright young woman, she is always making witty quips [comments].

Plot

The entire story revolves around plaid [a color pattern] overnight cases that are accidentally switched [exchanged] by their owners. One case belongs to a spy and contains secret government documents. Another one belongs to a rich older woman and is full of expensive jewelry. Judy has one too, with clothes and toiletries in it. Howard's is also exactly like the others and contains his collection of igneous rocks, which are a part of his research on prehistoric man's relationship to rocks and music.

Judy sees Howard check into the San Francisco Bristol Hotel and is immediately attracted to him. At a dinner party, and later, at a reception, she pretends to be his fiancée, Eunice. Dr. Laraby, of the Laraby Foundation, is enchanted with [is fascinated by] her wit and intellect. He decides to give Howard the $20,000 grant money. Meanwhile, hotel rooms are burning, overnight cases are getting switched, and one of the funniest chase scenes in the history of film takes place on the hilly streets of San Francisco.

Notes

- Elements of romantic comedy in this film:

(1) Mistaken identity—(a) Judy pretends to be Eunice, so everyone thinks Judy is Eunice; (b) Judy calls Howard "Steve"; (c) the overnight cases are mistakenly switched; (d) Eunice is given the wrong address of the reception.

(2) Strong woman/weak male—Judy and Howard, or Eunice and Howard. More specifically, this film is like a subgenre of the old romantic comedy. In that genre the weak man was sometimes an absent-minded professor or a researcher interested only in his studies. Two excellent examples are: *Bringing Up Baby* (1938) and *The Lady Eve* (1941).
(3) The dizzy female character—Judy is always causing accidents
(4) Funny, crazy, unbelievable scenes
(5) Snappy [fast and humorous] dialogue—Judy, in particular, has a quick, witty reply for everyone and is knowledgeable about many subjects, having been a student in probably a dozen universities.
(6) Love triangle—Judy-Howard-Eunice

Theme

- This film is in many ways similar to the traditional romantic comedy; thus the audience knows that, in the end, the crazy couple will go off together and continue to be nonconformists. They will not have home and family but will study, travel, and have crazy adventures. The theme seems to be one of breaking with traditional values. This is a typical theme of movies in the 1970s.

Previewing Questions
Moonstruck

1. What kinds of love are portrayed in this truly romantic comedy?
2. Review what you know of the Italian or Italian American culture. How does this film comically stereotype them?

Moonstruck

(1987) dir. Norman Jewison 104 min.
Starring: Cher [Best Actress Oscar], Nicolas Cage, Olympia Dukakis [Best Supporting Actress Oscar]

Setting: New York City

Characters

Loretta [Cher]—an accountant. She's a widow who believes she brings bad luck to relationships, especially because she and her husband were married in a civil ceremony rather than in a church ceremony. Her husband was struck and killed by a bus seven years ago.

Johnny Cammareri [Danny Aiello]—an Italian American small-business man. He is self-absorbed [egocentric], boring, and a "mother's boy."

Ronny Cammareri [Nicolas Cage]—Johnny's younger brother, a baker. He lost his hand in an accident at work. Since then he's had a bad attitude toward life. He blames Johnny for what happened to him. There is "bad blood" [bad feelings] between them.

Cosmo [Vincent Gardenia]—Loretta's father. He is a plumber and a good salesman. He prides himself on his ability to sell. He is obsessed [very worried] with growing old and dying. He has a girlfriend.

Rose [Olympia Dukakis]—Loretta's mother. She is very down-to-earth, very practical. She doesn't believe in love: love makes people crazy. She's glad that Loretta isn't in love with Johnny.

Grandfather—of Loretta, father of Cosmo. He believes that the moon brings the woman to the man. His character helps to convey the theme. The moon is the light of love. All the characters speak fondly of the moon: "la bella luna" (the beautiful moon). Love makes the world go around. Everyone is searching for completion, for love.

Plot

Loretta and Johnny are planning to be married as soon as his mother dies. She's very ill, and Johnny goes to Palermo, Italy, to visit and be with her in her final days. He tells Loretta that while he's gone he would like for her to convince Ronny, his brother, to come to the wedding and stop the fight they've been having with each other for years. Loretta goes to Ronny's bakery to ask him to attend the wedding. Although he is very hostile [unfriendly], they fall in love. The rest of the film concerns the resolution [happy conclusion] of this love triangle and offers a demonstration of the power of the moon and of the many different kinds of love that exist.

Notes

- The theme song "That's Amore" [That's Love] helps set the humorous and romantic tone. The opening scene of the Metropolitan Opera House at night also adds to the romantic mood.

- Italian culture in its stereotypical form is very evident throughout this film:

    —Funerals are important gathering places. Old people meet in the cemetery to reminisce [remember the old days] or to have discussions. Death is a friend to them, and family memories don't end with death.
    —Women look after men as they would children. They tell them what to wear, what to eat. They try to control them.
    —Johnny believes that a man who can't control his woman is laughable. This indicates that although women have the control, men perceive themselves as being in charge.
    —Italians are old-fashioned romantics. For instance, Loretta wants Johnny to kneel in front of her when he proposes marriage.
    —Loretta believes, as Catholics often do, that the wedding must be in the church or there will be bad luck in the marriage.
    —Italians get emotional easily. For example, their anger suddenly shows itself and they scream at each other and ask God to curse the people they're angry with. They are very intense [emotional] about life.
    —Loretta's family is the traditional extended family. The father works, the mother is a homemaker, the children live at home and have the option of continuing to live there even after they marry, and the grandparents also live in the home.
    —Italian men and women tend to exaggerate. To illustrate, when Ronny hears that his brother is going to be married, he threatens to cut his own throat [kill himself] because he feels that he, by comparison to his brother, has no life.
    —Religion (Catholicism) is important. After committing a major sin Catholics go to the priest to confess and receive God's forgiveness.
    —Family matters, both public and private, are discussed at meals. Nothing is secret. For instance, Rose tells her husband, in front of the family and a complete stranger (Ronny), to stop seeing his girlfriend. Then Ronny and Johnny have a personal conversation in front of Loretta's family. This is all perfectly natural.

- By the 1980s there were very few similarities to the romantic comedy of the 1930s and 1940s. What remains is basically

    (a) the love triangle: Johnny-Loretta-Ronny and Rose-Cosmo-Mona
    (b) snappy dialogue, especially from Loretta and her mother
    (c) strong, wise women and weaker, dependent men

- The name of the salon where Loretta goes to have her hair done is the Cinderella Beauty Salon. Loretta is transformed [changed] by love, just as Cinderella was transformed by her fairy godmother, after which she found her Prince Charming.

Themes

- There are many different kinds of love represented in this film, and they all mirror the theme of the complexities of love:

    —Johnny and his mother.
    —Ronny and the girl who works for him at the bakery. She has a crush on [likes] him, but he isn't interested. This is unrequited [impossible] love.
    —Loretta's aunt and uncle. They are an old couple, but they can still be playful about love.
    —Rose and Cosmo. An old married couple who have grown accustomed to each other; they're a habit. He cheats on her but she first accepts it and then asks him to stop.
    —Johnny and Loretta. A safe, practical love.
    —Loretta and Ronny. Wild, passionate, intense love.
    —Cosmo and Mona; and the man in the restaurant and his student lovers. The affairs of Cosmo and the professor represent the love of confused, aging men.

- The word *luna* translates into English as *moon*. Our English word *lunacy* is a derivation of the word. It means craziness, insanity. Hundreds of years ago people believed the full moon caused insanity. Love makes people a little crazy.

- Ronny's speech to Loretta about love is probably representative of the film's views on love. He tells her that love isn't really as nice as in the fairy tales; it destroys everything and everyone. He believes, however, that one of the reasons people are alive is to experience love, to ruin themselves by choosing the wrong lover, and then to die of a broken heart.

- Rose keeps asking why men chase women, and the answer she often gets is that men fear death. In other words, love keeps a man feeling young and alive. This idea is a subtheme.

Chapter 6
Hitchcock Films: The Auteur Genre

The auteur [author] approach to film study involves reviewing, describing, and analyzing all the major films of one director. The auteur critic looks for several elements in the auteur's films: the director's personal philosophy of life, the use of the same crew [group of workers] and the same cast members [actors], similar plots or themes or characters. Also to be considered is biographical and autobiographical information, as well as personal interviews with and articles written about the director (Bywater and Sobchack 1989, 51–54). To achieve the special status accorded an auteur is a great accomplishment. Other directors who are also in this auteur category include Charlie Chaplin, George Cukor, D. W. Griffith, Elia Kazan, David Lynch, Martin Scorsese, François Truffaut, and Billy Wilder.

Alfred Hitchcock (1899–1980) is still one of the best-known directors in the world, and his directing style continues to be studied and imitated. He had the unique ability to tell a story through the lens of a camera and to make his audiences feel and experience exactly what the characters were feeling and experiencing. We, the audience, are voyeurs, Peeping Toms, who are looking in on the private lives of the characters. But he also shows us that the visual can be deceiving [tricky]. Through his films he seems to be saying to us that nothing, no one, no place is absolutely safe, and nothing is what it seems to be. In fact he encourages paranoia in the audience.

To appreciate him as the great director he was, one must understand the various components [aspects] of his style. The most important aspect of his films is the visual, the sense of sight. Hitchcock lets the audience see how the characters are reacting. He accomplishes this by running together many subjective and reaction shots. In a subjective shot the camera is the character, so that we see what the character sees and thus we identify more strongly with that character, experiencing what she or he feels and sees. A reaction shot is defined by its name. The camera shows us how a character is reacting to what is happening.

Another aspect of Hitchcock's style that distinguishes him is the fact that he worked almost exclusively in the mystery/suspense genre. Other auteurs have worked in more than one genre successfully. For instance Billy Wilder made excellent comedies as well as dramas, but Hitchcock did his finest work within the suspense genre.

The dialogue among the characters also has a distinct [unique] Hitchcockian flavor. There is always much innuendo [something implied rather than stated], usually of an erotic, violent, or disturbing nature. Even so, there is also always something funny, something humorous in each film.

Basic to Hitchcock's style is the lack of a moral tone. There is no absolute right or wrong; there are only questions. His films don't illustrate traditional social values. Many of his main characters are bad guys, but we feel sympathy for them because Hitchcock does not make judgments about them (Sinyard 1986, 149). Ultimately good wins over evil, but the films are fascinating because they demonstrate the great power of evil. Stability is returned at the end of each film, but the uncertainty of that stability is made very clear (152). This characteristic is imitated by horror movies today. Often they end happily, but the characters don't realize that the evil thing is not gone and can still threaten [endanger] them in a movie sequel [part 2, part 3, etc.].

Hitchcock's style of directing is classic and orderly. When he was making a film, every detail had to be perfect. Note, for example, the opening scene of *Psycho*: across the screen is printed the date, time, and place of the action. In his careful attention to detail he often drew beforehand every camera shot in a scene from the angle and depth at which he wished it to be filmed, making the cameraperson's work very easy. Every shadow and every light had meaning. The lighting set the mood and tone, and the mood was usually one of suspense. As Hitchcock himself once said, "Suspense is like a woman. The more left to the imagination, the more the excitement" (Sinyard 1986, 7).

When studying an auteur one can see certain personal touches that distinguish that director's work and are like an artist's signature. With Hitchcock the personal touch was his cameo appearance in many of his films—that is he often appeared in a certain scene or with a certain character to emphasize a theme or image that was integral [significant] to the plot of that film. For instance, in *North by Northwest* he is seen getting on a bus. The emphasis is on travel and movement, which are central to the film. In *Notorious* he appears at the champagne table, letting the audience know that they should pay attention to drinking in all its various forms in the film.

Hitchcock very often used the same film crew, the same music composer (Bernard Herrmann), and a number of the same actors, including Cary Grant, Gregory Peck, James Stewart, Farley Granger, Grace Kelly, Ingrid Bergman, and Tippi Hedren. He also cast his daughter Patricia, a very minor actress, in two of his films: *Psycho* and *Strangers on a Train.*

Hitchcock's characters often speak in sexual undertones and innuendo [suggestion]. When, for instance, in the spy thriller *North by Northwest*, Roger Thornhill meets Eve Kendall in the dining car on the train, there is a lot of playful dialogue (compliments of writer Ernest Lehman), the implication being that they will get together later in her compartment for a sexual rendezvous [meeting]. The dialogue between Marion Crane and Norman Bates of *Psycho* is equally revealing of character. In reference to his relationship with his mother, Norman confesses to her that a mother is a son's best friend, while also admitting that a son is a poor substitute for a lover. Although it is true that in Hitchcock the visual is key to his work, it is also just as true that his characters reveal [show] to us their darker side through dialogue. Moreover, kisses are just as expressive in Hitchcock as dialogue. They tend to reflect the relationship between the characters. In *Rear Window*, Lisa covers Jeff's face with kisses while he remains unmoved. And Roger Thornhill kisses Eve in *North by Northwest* while holding her head as if to smash it (Wood 1977, 35).

Many auteurs have certain motifs [themes] that they employ again and again in their films. Hitchcock incorporated some of his own fears into his work. For example, there is his fear of the police. In *Psycho* the huge close-ups of the police officer and of private detective Arbogast are included to help us share his fear. In fact, in almost all of his films we are reminded that the police are powerless to help in times of crisis. Not only are the police powerless, they are also incompetent [not qualified], often chasing or arresting the wrong person, as in *North by Northwest*, *The Man Who Knew Too Much*, and *The Wrong Man*. Hitchcock's disrespect is particularly observable in *Rear Window* in the animosity [dislike] Jeffries has for policeman Tom Doyle. Other phobias [fears] of his, such as his fear of high places and falling, are evident in films such as *Vertigo*, *North by Northwest*, *Rear Window*, and *Spellbound*. Another motif, that of woman as victim, is played over and over. Some examples include Marion Crane of

Psycho, Alicia Huberman of *Notorious*, Eve Kendall of *North by Northwest*, Rebecca of the film by that name, and Ingrid Bergman's character in both *Under Capricorn* and *Notorious*. The peculiarities of the parent-child relationship are also a recurring theme: *Psycho*'s Norman and his mother, *North by Northwest*'s Roger Thornhill and his mother, *Notorious*'s Alicia Huberman and her Nazi spy father, and so on.

Previewing Questions
Notorious

1. What is the definition of *notorious*? Who among the characters fits this definition?
2. Note the many close-ups of bottles, cups, wine glasses, and the act of drinking itself. How is this emphasis important to the story and to the theme?
3. This film is more than a spy story. It concerns hidden emotions. Who is hiding what, and why?

Notorious

(1946) dir. Alfred Hitchcock 102 min.
Starring: Cary Grant, Ingrid Bergman, Claude Rains

Setting: A courthouse in Miami, Florida, April 24, 1946. John Huberman is sentenced to twenty years in prison for war crimes as a Nazi spy. Later setting: Rio de Janeiro, Brazil.

Characters

Alicia Huberman [Ingrid Bergman]—the daughter of the Nazi spy. She is being watched by the U.S. government officials, who think she may have been his accomplice [partner].

Devlin [Cary Grant]—an agent with the U.S. government. He has been authorized to convince Alicia to go to Rio de Janeiro, Brazil, on a mission to spy on her father's friends who have a spy ring there.

Paul Prescott [Louis Calhern]—Devlin's boss. He is on the plane to Rio the day after the trial. He and Dev and Alicia spend more than a week there preparing her for the mission and waiting for her orders to arrive.

Alexander Sebastian [Claude Rains]—the leader of the German spy ring in Rio and in the past a good friend and associate of Alicia's father. Although much older than Alicia, he had, at the time of his association with her father, been in love with her. Ultimately, however, she rejected him. Prescott wants Alicia to get to know Alex again and to visit his house so that she can monitor his activities.

Madame Sebastian [Leopoldine Konstantin]—Alex's mother. She is extremely attached to her son, who is middle aged and still living at home, allowing his mother to dominate him. She is immediately suspicious [doubtful] of Alicia because she is, of course, jealous of any woman who attracts her son's attention and because she knows that Alicia didn't testify for her father at his trial.

Plot

After Alicia meets Alex while horseback riding, he invites her to his home for a dinner party. This is precisely what Prescott wanted. She is supposed to spy on the spies. There is an incident during the dinner: Emile, one of the German spies, suddenly acts very nervous when he sees one of the wine bottles that are to be opened for dinner. He thinks there is something else in the bottles. Among the people Alicia meets at the party is a Dr. Anderson, whose real name, Prescott later tells her, is Wilhelm Otto Renssler. He is doing scientific research at Alex Sebastian's house.

Soon Sebastian asks Alicia to marry him. When she reports this event to Prescott, he thinks this is a perfect arrangement. Now she will be able to live in the house and keep the U.S. officials informed of all the activities of the spies. Prescott wants to know what kind of research is being conducted.

After their marriage, Alicia investigates the house. She discovers that she can't get into the wine cellar. Alex has the key. She tells Dev, who tells her to throw a party and invite him so that he can try to get into the wine cellar during the confusion of the party. Before the party Alicia steals the key to the wine cellar from Alex's key ring and slips [passes] it to Dev when he arrives. When Dev visits the wine cellar, he accidentally breaks a wine bottle and discovers that it contains some kind of metal ore. Alex later discovers the breakage and knows then that Alicia is an American agent. If his German spy friends find out, they will kill him just as they killed Emile when he made the mistake at the dinner party. His mother suggests an "illness" that will slowly kill Alicia. Everyone will then think that she died naturally and no one will know that Alex was married to a spy.

Eventually Alicia realizes that Alex and his mother are poisoning her, but by then it is too late. She's too sick to help herself. When Alicia doesn't show up for her meetings with Dev for five days, Dev gets suspicious and comes for a visit to Alex's house.

He finds Alicia and finally declares his love for her, which is all she wanted to hear. He takes her away in front of Alex and all Alex's German agents. Of course Alex will be murdered by all his colleagues because they will figure out what's going on, especially since Alex doesn't go to the hospital with Alicia.

Notes

- Consider the meaning of the word *notorious*. Anyone who is notorious is well known and talked about; in fact, that person is usually unfavorably spoken of. At the film's beginning Alicia is the notorious one, as is her father. But other characters are notorious in their own way.

- *Notorious* was one of the three most popular thrillers of the 1940s, along with two other Hitchcock films: *Suspicion* and *Spellbound* (Sinyard 1986, 43).

- *Notorious* is a good example of how carefully Hitchcock constructed his plots and scenes. The first sequences [scenes] in the film appear again at the end of the film, in reverse. In the beginning: (*a*) there is an open door and three men and a judge; (*b*) Alicia leaves the courtroom, alone;

(c) at the party there is talk of drinking and love; (d) Dev and Alicia leave her house. She is too drunk to walk steadily and he puts a scarf around her for warmth. The police go away after Dev shows his identification; (e) Alicia has a hangover and can't see well in the bright morning light. At the film's end: (a) Alicia can't see well because of the poison and the darkroom; (b) Alicia and Dev get ready to leave her house and she can't walk steadily because of the poison. Dev puts his coat around her. He protects her from the men by hiding his identity; (c) Alicia and Dev speak of poison and of love; (d) Alicia leaves her house, not alone but with Dev; (e) there is the open door of the house and one man (Alex) standing before three judges (his associates) (Spoto 1992, 150–51).

- There is much emphasis in this film on drinking. The camera often focuses on glasses and bottles and people drinking: there are alcoholic drinks, tea, coffee, champagne. Hitchcock makes his cameo appearance at the party in front of the champagne table. There is also much talk of Alicia's drinking problem. The metal ore is hidden in wine bottles. The poison is concealed in tea. The theme of drinking is a complex one, motivating characters and moving the plot forward (Sinyard 1986, 64). Further, it seems clear that drinking is to be viewed negatively. The characters drink to escape reality and unhappiness. And the liquid itself is, in one case, literally poison (Spoto 1992, 148–49).

- This film was made in 1946, just after World War Two. The Germans are portrayed as evil and secretive and quick to murder their own agents if mistakes are made. Hitchcock was British, and the film was made in the United States, so it would be easy to assume that the film would be overly biased [prejudiced] in favor of the Allies. In fact, Hitchcock is fairly nonjudgmental. The American agents are not much more sympathetic than their Fascist counterparts. Both groups take unfair advantage of poor Alicia.

- Although Alicia is the primary protagonist who elicits [attracts] our sympathy, Alex also is a character with whom the audience can identify. The reason is that both are victims. Alicia is the victim of a spy father and the pawn [servant] of the CIA [Central Intelligence Agency]. Alex is dominated by his mother, his attachment to Alicia, and his contacts [associates] in the Nazi spy ring (Wood 1989, 306–7).

- Alicia has a need for surrogate [substitute] fathers. Alex is much older than she and is a kind of father figure. "Dr. Anderson" is another father figure. When Alicia says to the doctor "Oh, you're leaving? I'll miss you," she is serious. Besides, Dr. Anderson's role as a compassionate man helps to confuse the audience more about the good guys and the bad guys. Both sets of spies have some good qualities (Spoto 1992, 153–55).

- There are many contrasts in *Notorious*: (*a*) Alicia acts like a promiscuous [free with sexual favors] woman and the CIA uses her as a sexual lure [attraction], but what she really wants is true love; (*b*) when she later appears to be drunk, she has actually been poisoned; (*c*) Alex and his mother and the Nazi spies always act civil and socially correct, but in reality they are murderers; (*d*) wine bottles contain not wine but uranium ore; (*e*) Dev loves Alicia but acts as if he does not; (*f*) Alex and his mother appear to be very concerned about Alicia's health but are in fact poisoning her (Spoto 1992, 153).

Themes

- This is not just a spy thriller but rather a study of certain themes: trust and losing trust, loyalty and trickery, and the highs and lows of love.

- Parental love is presented as problematic: (*a*) Alicia both loves and hates her Nazi father; (*b*) Sebastian's mother controls him and is jealous of Alicia (Sinyard 1986, 64).

- The central story of *Notorious* is not that of spies and uranium ore; it is Alicia and Dev. Both of these characters are very needy. Alicia needs to feel that Dev trusts her and believes in her love. She has had a sad life and feels guilty about her relationship with her spy father. Dev is also needy, but it is difficult for him to make a commitment to love because he has spent his professional life hiding his emotions. He can't trust himself to show love, nor can he trust Alicia to be faithful to him. The entire film is about hidden emotions (Spoto 1992, 148).

Previewing Questions
Rear Window

1. What similarities do you see between *Rear Window* and *Moonstruck*? In what ways is this Hitchcock version a darker study?
2. What is a *Peeping Tom*? Is it ethical to spy on one's neighbors if, in doing so, you can help them? Or is the act of spying always an invasion of privacy?
3. Each director/auteur has certain unique trademarks [symbols] that are recognizable to the audience. Hitchcock's cameo appearances in his films are one of his directorial idiosyncrasies [habits]. In what scene does Hitchcock make his cameo appearance?

Rear Window

(1954) dir. Alfred Hitchcock 112 min.
Starring: Grace Kelly, James Stewart

Setting: some apartment buildings in New York City, midsummer

Characters

L. B. (Jeff) Jeffries [James Stewart]—a photojournalist who has been out of work for seven weeks with a broken leg. He enjoys traveling on assignment because he can avoid marriage. He is very insecure and uncertain about whether or not to marry.

Stella [Thelma Ritter]—the housekeeper/nurse. She offers Jeff a lot of practical advice.

Lisa Fremont [Grace Kelly]—a society girl who works in a very expensive dress shop on Park Avenue. She wants Jeff to quit his job, which takes him all over the world, and instead to get one as a businessman in New York so that they can be married.

Tom Doyle [Wendell Corey]—a police buddy of Jeff's. He and Jeff were in World War Two together.

Characters from the apartment complex

Miss Lonely Hearts—an older, unmarried woman who is lonely and wants love.

Miss Torso—the ballet dancer who has lots of boyfriends, none serious.

The Honeymooners—a newlywed couple who never come out of their apartment.

The Songwriter—a middle-aged, unmarried, lonely composer who spends his days composing love songs on the piano.

Mr. and Mrs. Lars Thorwald—an older, costume jewelry salesman and his invalid wife. They argue a lot.

An older couple—who sleep out on the fire escape to stay cool and who also have a dog.

Miss Hearing Aids—an older woman, unmarried or widowed, perhaps, who is a sculptress.

Plot

Jeff spends every day bound to his wheelchair, bored and uncomfortable. To entertain himself, he watches the neighbors and follows the pattern of their daily lives. He even gives some of them pet names. He doesn't know any of them personally, so he invents names for them. For example, one woman who lives alone seems always to be searching for romance, so he calls her "Miss Lonely Hearts." One night, unable to sleep because of the heat, he notices that the salesman across the courtyard leaves his apartment three times, each time carrying with him a suitcase. After watching him carefully for a few days, and seeing that the salesman's invalid wife has disappeared, Jeff begins to think that she has been murdered by her husband. Most of the film revolves around Jeff's attempt to prove that his suspicion is right.

Notes

- The musical score is composed entirely of love songs, so the music acts as an indicator of the theme. The importance of music is made particularly clear on two occasions: (*a*) when Hitchcock makes his cameo appearance in the musician's apartment, thus reminding the audience to pay attention to the music; and (*b*) when, upon hearing the musician's song, Miss Lonely Hearts decides not to commit suicide. Additionally, as we see Hitchcock standing in the musician's apartment, he is not just listening to the music; he is resetting the man's clock. Time is also an important element in this film (Sragow 1994, 153).

- This film is a metaphor for the experience of watching a film. The apartments across the square from Jeff represent the movie screen, and Jeff is a filmgoer who "projects his own fantasies on to the characters he sees, identifying with some, rejecting others, but most importantly, hoping to be entertained and excited by what he sees" (Sinyard 1986, 85).

- Subconsciously [without really being aware of it], Jeff is very much afraid of commitment and of getting married. It is clear throughout the film that he can't decide whether being single means being lonely or being free. Further, he is unable to conclude whether being married will bring him happiness and peace or will be like prison to him.

- There are many contrasts in this movie, a fact we can see reflected in the lives of the neighbors. Miss Torso, surrounded by her many admirers, contrasts dramatically with the lonely spinster, Miss Lonely Hearts. A newly married couple contrasts with Thorwald and his invalid wife, who argue with and hate each other. From his window, Jeff sees many kinds of love: frustrated love [Miss Lonely Hearts], displaced love [the old couple and their dog/child], lack of love [Miss Hearing Aids], love that has just begun [the newlyweds], and love replaced by hate [Thorwald and his wife]. Seeing all this just makes him more confused about whether or not to marry. His Peeping Tom behavior is just a way of delaying the time when he will have to search his own soul in order to understand himself better (Sinyard 1986, 85).

- Jeff uses his camera to keep life at a comfortable distance without getting too involved. He watches but does not participate. In the confrontation with Thorwald, however, we see how ineffective [useless] the camera is. The message seems to be that Jeff must make decisions and interact in the real world (Wood 1989, 105).

- As is true with many Hitchcock films, the ending appears to be a happy one, but the happiness is superficial [not deep] because the problems haven't really been solved. Jeff has his back to the window in the last scene (but for how long?) and Lisa appears to be reading an adventure book, when in reality she is hiding a fashion magazine, *Harper's Bazaar*. The other people living in the apartments seem to live happily ever after, too. Notice what happens to each of them (Wood 1989, 106).

Themes

- The first and most significant theme is reflected not only in Jeff's relationship with Lisa but also in the film's music and in all the characters of the apartment complex. It concerns the issues of love and marriage, compatibility [getting along together], and the nature of male-female relationships. Given the ending, it appears that Hitchcock's own views were rather cynical, especially considering the fact that all the neighbors except the newlyweds seem to be happy.

- Stella tells Jeff, "We've become a race of Peeping Toms. What people ought to do is get outside their own house and look in for a change!" (Spoto 1992, 222). Jeff is a Peeping Tom, and thus the second theme concerns the question of whether voyeurism [spying on people] is or is not ethical [moral]. In fact Jeff, at one point, says to Lisa, "I wonder if it's ethical to watch a man with binoculars and a long-focus lens. Do you suppose it's ethical even if you prove he didn't commit a crime?" (222).

- A third theme deals with involvement. Jeff sees life through his camera but does not participate actively. The same behavior holds in his relationship with Lisa. The point seems to be that neighbors (and men and women) should interact. The older woman whose dog is murdered tells everyone that she believes that neighbors should like each other, should speak to one another, and should be concerned for each other's well being.

Previewing Questions
North by Northwest

1. Review the section entitled "The Auteur Genre." What recurring Hitchcock motifs do you find in *North by Northwest*?
2. Love is difficult for the male protagonists in Hitchcock films. What seems to be Roger Thornhill's problem?
3. The character of Roger Thornhill is changed as he moves north by northwest across the United States. How is his an inner journey as well?

North by Northwest
(1959) dir. Alfred Hitchcock   136 min.
Starring: Cary Grant, Eva Marie Saint

Setting: This film is like a travelogue for the U.S. tourist industry as the main character moves from New York City in a northwesterly direction to the state of South Dakota.

Characters

Roger O. Thornhill [Cary Grant]—a Madison Avenue advertising man, handsome and charming to the ladies. Although he is very proper and sophisticated, he has his negative side. He is sarcastic, shallow [superficial], selfish, and irresponsible. He has a tendency to drink too much. He has been divorced twice.

"Townsend"/Vandamm [James Mason]—the head of a spy ring that is selling U.S. government secrets and documents to the Communists. Townsend is just an assumed [false] name. The real Townsend is a prominent [well-known] man at the United Nations.

Leonard [Martin Landau]—one of Vandamm's men. Leonard is his most valued and trusted assistant.

Thornhill's mother [Jessie Royce Landis]—a silly, vapid [empty-headed] old woman. Thornhill seems very attached to her. She is as shallow as he is, and only interested in fashion, the theatre, and card games like bridge.

Eve Kendall [Eva Marie Saint]—supposedly an industrial designer, although her real assignment is to be a spy. She helps Thornhill escape from the police by hiding him in her compartment on the train. She is a very sensual character, like many of Hitchcock's other female leads.

Plot

Thornhill, mistaken for a secret agent named George Kaplan, is kidnapped by spies and taken to a large estate to be questioned about how much he knows about their spy ring. This group has been following Kaplan for months although they've never actually seen him; they just know what hotels Kaplan has been staying in. Thornhill, whom they believe to be Kaplan, refuses to tell them anything. (Because in reality, he doesn't know anything.) They get him drunk, put him in a car, and hope he will have a fatal accident. He survives, is put in jail for drunk driving, and no one believes his story about being kidnapped. When the police go to the estate to investigate Thornhill's story, "Mrs. Townsend" lies about everything. To prove he is right, Roger first takes his mother to Kaplan's hotel room to talk to him, in order to clear up the confusion. They can't find Kaplan but they get into his room to investigate. While they are in the room, a call comes through. Thornhill answers it. It's from the men who tried to kill him the night before. Of course now they have no doubt that he's Kaplan. Two of the spies chase him from the hotel. Thornhill goes to the United Nations to talk to Townsend. That's when he discovers that the "Townsend" he met wasn't the real one. As he begins to speak with the real Townsend, one of the spies kills him. Everyone at the U.N. thinks Thornhill (Kaplan) did it. He has to run away, and for the remainder of the movie he must continue to run, not only from the killer spies but also from the police, who think he is a murderer. We find out that the CIA "created" Kaplan, that Kaplan doesn't really exist. He is just a decoy [substitute] to attract the spies so that the CIA can capture them and prevent them from stealing any more government secrets. When the CIA agents discover that Thornhill has been mistaken for Kaplan, they can't help him. If they do help him, their own CIA spy will be put in danger. On his own, with everyone chasing him, Thornhill moves gradually across the United States, in a northwesterly direction, looking for Kaplan and a way to clear his own name.

Notes

- In this film many of Hitchcock's recurring motifs are present:
    (a) the problem of identity (as in *Psycho*)
    (b) a fear of sudden death (as in *Psycho*) (Sinyard 1986, 112)
    (c) a love triangle (as in *Notorious*)
    (d) the selfish, inconsiderate use of individuals by government spies in an attempt to get power and information (as in *Notorious*) (Sinyard 1986, 108)
    (e) dramatic contrasts (as in *Psycho*): The normal hotel lobby is the setting for kidnapping, the United Nations for murder, farmlands for a crop-dusting plane's attempt to shoot down the protagonist, and Mount Rushmore for a dangerous chase (Sinyard 1986, 104).
    (f) the uselessness of the police (as in *Psycho* and *Rear Window*) (Sinyard 1986, 109)
    (g) the fear of heights and falling (as in *Rear Window*)
    (h) the peculiar parent-child relationship (as in *Psycho* and *Notorious*)

- Other motifs not necessarily recurrent in Hitchcock include the journey motif. As Thornhill moves across the United States we see his progress toward becoming a better man (Spoto 1992, 303). And there is an emphasis on the hands. In the train compartment Thornhill and Eve make interesting and suggestive movements with their hands, and in the concluding scenes the hands are lifesavers (Chase 1994, 64).

- Like *Notorious*, *North by Northwest* clearly shows that politics and spies are just as bad on both sides. Just as Alicia was used by the American spies in *Notorious*, Roger Thornhill is used by the Washington agents as bait to capture the spy master they're looking for. To them, people like Thornhill are expendable [replaceable]. In fact, Eve Kendall, a double agent, is just as expendable to the Washington spies as Roger is (Spoto 1992, 301, 303).

- Hitchcock was obsessed with details but also had a sense of humor. The number 13 is unlucky in this culture, and poor Eve Kendall, the double agent, has the bad luck to be used by both spy groups. She is associated with the number 13 in this film. For instance she's in car 3901 on the train (3 + 9 + 0 + 1 = 13), and she's in room 463 (4 + 6 + 3 = 13) at the hotel in Chicago (Spoto 1992, 308).

- Consider the interesting undertones. For example, what are we to think about Thornhill's two failed marriages and his close relationship to his mother? And what about Leonard? Is he in love with Vandamm? He mentioned his "woman's intuition" and seemed very jealous of Eve. And why are all of Hitchcock's female leads so "easy," so free with their sexual favors?

Themes

- There is the search for truer and deeper identity. Roger Thornhill is a sophisticated but emotionally empty playboy and businessman. (His initials signal this: R.O.T.) In his rise to success in the advertising world, which is in itself a very shallow and deceptive business, he has lost his humanity, his ability to feel. This film chronicles [follows] his return to being human again.

- Another theme is the building of a relationship. As in *Notorious*, the male lead must overcome his inability to exhibit emotions. He must learn to care about and love a woman.

- A third theme criticizes a world in which everything and everyone is phony [false, not real]. For instance, Roger Thornhill is in advertising and has been lying all of his professional life. Further, spying includes lying and hiding identities. The characters lie and steal and change names and identities. The values are not deep; there are no moral convictions. Every spy must do what is best at that moment. People are expendable. Many of the characters themselves are phony. Kaplan, for example, doesn't exist, Vandamm is masquerading [pretending to be] Townsend, Roger Thornhill is thought to be Kaplan, and Eve Kendall is a double agent. Even the bullets used to "kill" Roger are fake (Spoto 1992, 303–4).

Previewing Questions
Psycho

1. The dialogue is filled with many references to family. Why?
2. Secrets are also a subtheme in this film. How many of the characters, both major and minor, have something to hide?
3. What is the symbolic importance of the birds, the frequent focus of the camera on the eyes, the cellar, the circles and holes, the mirrors, Norman's room, and the Victorian decor of Norman's house?

Psycho

(1960) dir. Alfred Hitchcock   120 min.
Starring: Anthony Perkins, Janet Leigh, Vera Miles, John Gavin

Setting: Phoenix, Arizona, Friday, December 11, 2:43 P.M.; later: Fairvale, California

Characters

Marion Crane [Janet Leigh]—the young, orphaned secretary who steals money from the real estate agency where she works in order to be with her lover.

Sam Loomis [John Gavin]—Marion's fiancé who lives far away in Fairvale, California, and who cannot marry her because he has insufficient funds. He runs a hardware store and is trying to pay off his debts and his ex-wife.

Norman Bates [Anthony Perkins]—the shy young man who runs the Bates Motel, which now has almost no customers since the main highway was moved. He lives in the old, ruined Gothic mansion behind the motel.

Lila Crane [Vera Miles]—Marion's sister and the person who initiates the search for Marion after she disappears.

Detective Arbogast [Martin Balsam]—the private investigator who is hired by the real estate agency to "quietly" find Marion and the money, thereby avoiding [preventing] a scandal.

Plot

The first half of the film revolves around Marion Crane, her life, her guilt, and her terrible fate. Then when the protagonist, Marion, is killed, the audience is forced to identify with Norman. The plot is now larger and includes his life, his guilt, and his fate. Ultimately the story line concerns the solving of the mystery of Marion's disappearance and of Norman's abnormal personality.

Psycho opens with the camera panning [moving across] a city view. Then we see the name of the city, an exact date, and the time, as the camera continues to move over the tops of buildings. It stops for a moment, seems to make a choice, focuses again, and finally "enters" a dark room. The camera seemingly has made an arbitrary selection. What this means is that "this could be any place, any date, any time, any room—it could be *us*" (Wood 1989, 142).

Notes

- This movie story line comes from a short novel by Robert Bloch (Spoto 1992, 314).

- There is much emphasis on money at first, but Hitchcock makes it clear that money is not of real importance, not even to Marion. To her, money is a means to an end, a way to get what she wants, which is a respectable life with Sam.

- Marion's behavior is beyond her control. There are numerous incidents to illustrate how impossible her plan is. Yet the audience wants her to succeed and actually identifies with her. This is achieved by Hitchcock through the use of a combination of <u>reaction shots</u> (the camera looks at the character's face to show us her reaction to something) and <u>subjective shots</u> (we see through the eyes of the character herself). We watch her desperate escape as she moves into the darkness by car to California, and even though we know her plan is impossible, we sympathize with her each step of her journey.

- Marion and Norman's meeting is probably the most significant segment of the movie. The two characters are parallel in certain ways. Just as she represents the normal, he is the abnormal; while her behavior is compulsive, his is psychotic. Each is a prisoner. Norman tells her that every person has a private trap, a "psychological hell." Marion understands what Norman means; she recognizes the trap that she has put herself into. This is clear from her conversation with Norman. When he says, "We all go a little mad [crazy] sometimes. Haven't you?" she answers, "Sometimes just one time can be enough. Thank you." And she determines to go back to Phoenix and return the money. This decision gives her back her freedom; she is in control again and is able to behave like a logical human being. Thus in the shower scene, having decided to go back, she is washing away her guilt (Wood 1989, 145–46).

- Hitchcock toys [plays] with the audience's ability to choose a main character with whom to identify. He kills off the protagonist in the first hour and therefore forces the audience to identify with Norman. Further, he makes sure that we have mixed feelings about both of these characters. We feel sorry for Marion—a woman without a family, yet we disapprove of her secret meetings with Sam. And Norman seems like such a nice young man that we want him to hide his mother's crime and wash away the evidence.

- Setting is crucial in establishing the atmosphere of the film. Among the many contrasts offered in this film is that of Bates Motel, a seedy [shabby, run-down] little nothing of a place, representative of Norman himself, and Norman's family home, an old Gothic mansion that towers over [dominates] the small motel and that represents Norman's mother. The stereotypical Gothic house represents, in itself, a kind of horror. Often the center of horror stories, such a house is usually the scene of murder and insanity. It contains hidden rooms or objects and dark family secrets.

- *Psycho* contains many important symbols:

  —*Victorian decor*—indicative of repressed sexuality (Wood 1989, 147). Victorians [people who lived during the reign of Queen Victoria of England:1837–1901] were extremely conservative; mention of anything sexual in nature was strictly forbidden. Growing up in this atmosphere, repressing [keeping inside] his natural desires, Norman has become warped [not normal].

  —*Birds*— give the illusion of life, but they are dead. Their eyes see nothing.

  —*Eyes*—the windows of the soul. They watch the guilty. Norman's mother watches over him in his paranoid state.

  —*Cellar*—symbolic of the womb. Norman hides his mother there.

  —*Circles and holes*—(for example—the peep hole, the drain, etc.) symbols of the opening of the reproductive organ of the female anatomy. Norman is preoccupied with all things female.

  —*Mirrors*—the most frequently employed motif in the film. The mirror is the symbol of two things: a split personality and the characters' attempts at introspection [trying to understand the inner self]. For instance, Marion checks her reflection in the mirror of the hotel room, in the office, at home—apparently trying to decide what to do. In many scenes a mirror splits [divides] the image of nearly every character, indicating indecision and insecurity—and foreshadowing the ending (Spoto 1992, 317–18).

  —*Norman's room*—symbol of his arrested [stopped] development, both emotional and mental (Wood 1989, 147).

  —*Shower murder*—symbolic of Norman's rape of Marion. It is a violent substitute for the sex act that Norman is too repressed to perform (Wood 1989, 148).

  —*References to family*—Family is emphasized strongly in *Psycho*. This is Hitchcock's way of telling the audience that the family unit is very fragile [easily broken]. Hitchcock shows us the consequences of family degeneration through the characters, making a joke of the value of the stable [reliable] American family and especially the holy role given to mothers. Family is mentioned from the very opening scenes: Sam and Marion discuss his ex-wife and dead father, her dead parents and her sister. At work her coworker Caroline [Hitchcock's daughter Patricia] refers to her mother and husband. The client Cassidy mentions his daughter's wedding. Norman is dominated by his mother, and the mother-child emphasis becomes even more profound [deep] when we consider that Norman's personality is totally destroyed by his mother (Wood 1989, 114–16).

- Note also the many contrasts: the small town normality of Fairvale and the crazy Norman Bates just outside of town; the horrible murder in the pure, white bathroom; the Gothic mansion [Mother] and the motel [Little Norman]; innocence and evil; city and country; money and sex. These contrasts demonstrate the big division between the real and the horrible.

- Understanding the psychiatrist's explanation of Norman's behavior is a little difficult. Basically Norman's mental instability had begun after his father's death, when Norman was about five years old. He lived an isolated life with his mother until sometime during his adolescence when his mother found a boyfriend. Norman was incredibly jealous of the attentions she paid to this man, so he killed them both with strychnine [a kind of poison]. As the psychiatrist explains it, matricide [the killing of one's mother] is the worst crime of all. Norman couldn't live with the guilt, so he tried to bring his mother back to life by talking in her voice and wearing her clothes. Sometimes his own personality completely disappeared and he actually became his mother, totally, but sometimes he was half Norman and half his mother. However, his guilt was so intense that he could never be only Norman. When he was sexually aroused [excited] by a woman, the mother-half became very jealous. Norman naturally assumed that his mother would be jealous of the attentions he received from women since he had been jealous of her lover. Thus the mother-half committed the murders, while the Norman-half was in almost a dream state.

- Note the huge close-up of (*a*) the policeman as he stares into Marion's car window and (*b*) Arbogast the detective as he stares through the window of Sam's hardware store. Recall Hitchcock's phobia of the police, of being wrongly accused of a crime and of going to jail an innocent man. He attempts to instill [put] in the audience this same fear with these giant close-ups.

- Other excellent films of this transvestite/suspense type include *Psycho IV*, in which we are able to discover more about Norman's youth, *Fatal Attraction*, which borrowed heavily from the themes and style of *Psycho*, and *Dressed to Kill*, which concerns another cross-dressing murderer.

Themes

- The past controls the present. For instance, Sam and Marion can't marry because of the debts of his now-dead father and the alimony he pays his ex-wife. Norman's behavior is also a product of his shadowy past (Wood 1989, 143).

- Secrets are a subtheme. The movie begins with Marion and Sam's meeting secretly. Marion steals money, and that fact must be kept secret. Norman, too, has deep secrets. Everyone has something hidden—even the minor characters. For example, Marion's coworker Caroline was hiding tranquilizers [drugs] on the day of their wedding; Cassidy (the man who pays $40,000 cash for a house for his daughter) hides some of his earnings so that he won't have to pay higher taxes; Marion's boss hides a whiskey bottle in his office, and Arbogast describes the Bates Motel by saying "This is the first place that looks like it's hiding from the world" (Spoto 1992, 316).

- As mentioned before, one important theme is that of the fragility of family relationships.

- Another point is that everything is not as it appears. What we see is only a half-truth—our perceptions can be wrong. Hitchcock makes this theme clear by using the motif of the dead, staring eyes (Spoto 1992, 314).

Chapter 7
Suspense Films

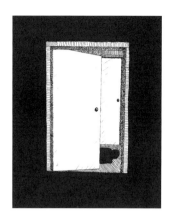

Hitchcock's favorite genre, of which he was the master in his day, was the suspense film. These days the classic suspense films are magnified in a new version of themselves called the *thriller*, which is complete with more blood, more violence, more sex, and more psychosis. Yet the thriller has its origins in the film noir of the 1940s and 1950s. (See chapter 2 for more details.) The noir films of that era were a reaction to the musicals and light comedy of the 1930s, and today, after the optimistic and superficial "feel good" movies of the 1980s, this return to noir reflects a growing sense that all is not well. The young, upwardly mobile professionals, or yuppies, have discovered that they cannot make the big money that their parents did. They are disillusioned with the myth of the comfortable middle class. The younger, recent college graduates are confronted with a shrinking job market. Cities have become overcrowded, violent, dangerous places. Even the police cannot be trusted; they are likely to be as corrupt as the criminals that inhabit the filthy cities.

As compared with the thrillers of the 1980s and 1990s, there are major differences in the old crime thrillers like *Double Indemnity* (1944), *Kiss of Death* (1947), Hitchcock's *Strangers on a Train* (1951), and even the post-noir *Charade* (1964). In the earlier era the bad guys often looked like criminals, and their main objective was to get money or revenge. These days the antagonists' motives are more varied, and they are often handsome, like Richard Gere's character in *Internal Affairs* (1990), or in excellent physical condition, like Robert De Niro's character in *Cape Fear*, or educated professionals like Eugene, the commodities broker in *Blue Steel* (1990) (Rainer 1994, 26–29).

135

Also different in the newer era of thriller movies is the extent to which the plot remains realistic. Whereas in the previous era the action was usually believable and logical, later films have exaggerated reality, making their heroes almost superhuman with the aid of special camera effects. In *Charade* (1964), for instance, the plot is fairly straightforward and the characters react as predicted. By the late 1980s and after (*D.O.A.*, *Cape Fear*, *Traces of Red*), the plot twists are more dramatic and frequent, the main characters survive numerous attacks by bad guys, and the level of violence is constant and breathtaking.

Despite the differences in the genre over time, there remain a striking number of similarities. The key elements of suspense itself are still very much present: the tension, anxiety, and sense of desperation are all integral parts of any suspense or thriller film. Further, the plot remains the single most important element of the genre. (For that reason the plot of each film in this chapter is discussed in great detail.) Usually there are many confusing twists to the story and many red herrings [clues or theories that are wrong or irrelevant] thrown in to fool the audience. Often in this genre the antagonist is a psycho, a deranged person whose psychosis may be hidden behind a professional exterior. Violence and murder are necessary ingredients, and often the reason for them is revenge. Romance, or in recent times sex, is usually required. In *Charade*, a product of the moral fiber of the 1950s and 1960s, romance is the order of the day. In later thrillers raw sex, violent and impersonal, is more frequently the case. In fact, women are usually mere victims and sex objects in recent thrillers, weak and helpless in the face of male aggression. All historical differences aside, the suspense/thriller genre is still alive and enjoying tremendous popularity.

Previewing Questions
Charade

1. What is a *charade*? In what ways is the narrative a charade?
2. This is an interesting film in that it has elements both of Hitchcock and of the romantic comedy. As in Hitchcock, for example, there is the spy motif and the male protagonist who has strong reservations about love. In what ways does it fit the romantic comedy genre?
3. The theme is one of trust. In what other films has this issue been important?

Charade

(1963) dir. Stanley Donen 113 min.
Starring: Cary Grant, Audrey Hepburn

Setting: the Swiss Alps, later: Paris, France

Characters

Regina (Reggie) Lampert [Audrey Hepburn]—a woman of leisure, unhappily married to a very secretive man named Charles.

Peter Joshua [Cary Grant]—a bright, handsome, older gentleman whom Regina meets while on vacation in the Swiss Alps.

Mr. Hamilton Bartholomew [Walter Matthau]—a high-ranking member of the CIA [Central Intelligence Agency].

Gideon [Ned Glass], Scobee (Herman) [George Kennedy], Tex [James Coburn]—the three bad guys.

Plot

Regina, vacationing in the Swiss Alps with her French friend Sylvie and Sylvie's little boy Jean Louis, is considering divorcing her husband. She is tired of all his lies and his secrets. During this vacation time she meets tall, good-looking Peter Joshua, to whom she is attracted.

Back in Paris, Regina is informed by the police of the death of her husband Charles. They claim he was thrown from a train. He was apparently in the process of leaving Reggie forever because he had sold all of their belongings at auction, for about $250,000, and had a ticket for Venezuela. The only possessions he had with him were inside a small carry-on bag. The contents included: a wallet containing 4,000 francs; an agenda book, the last appointment marked for Thursday, 5:00 P.M., at the Jardins des Champs-Elysées; the ticket to Venezuela; a letter, stamped but unsealed and addressed to Regina; a key to their apartment; a pen; a comb; and a toothbrush. Also in the bag were several passports for different countries, all containing Charles's picture but different names.

During the funeral service for Charles, a note comes to Regina asking her to appear at the American Embassy the next day. There she meets Mr. Bartholomew. He explains that her husband, whose real name was Vass, was an agent [spy] under observation by the CIA. Mr. Bartholomew warns her that she is in great danger from the three men whom she saw at the funeral. They all want the $250,000 that Charles had stolen. Mr. Bartholomew says the money actually belongs to the CIA.

Soon Mr. Bartholomew's predictions become reality. Each of the three men threatens Regina. Their stories, and Peter's, confuse her, so Regina calls Bartholomew for advice. He explains the whole story. He tells her that in 1944, during World War Two, the three men—Gideon, Scobee (Herman), and Tex—were in the OSS [the wartime version of the CIA] with her husband Charles and another man named Carson Dyle. These five men were ordered to go behind the German combat lines to deliver $250,000 in gold to the French underground. Instead of doing so, the five men stole and buried it. Before they could escape, however, the Germans attacked them. Herman lost his arm and Dyle supposedly was killed. After the war, Charles was the first man to go back and get the gold. Of course the others wanted it too. And the CIA, represented by Mr. Bartholomew, also wants it because technically it belongs to the CIA.

After explaining all this to Regina, Mr. Bartholomew tells her to find out as much as she can about the mysterious and charming Peter, who may in fact be Carson Dyle. Peter's story is that he is not Carson Dyle; he is Alexander or "Alex" Dyle, Carson's brother. Alex, formerly Peter, believes that Carson did not want to steal the money, and he is trying to prove that Carson was innocent so that the reputation of his dead brother will be saved.

Eventually Regina and Alex and the three men decide to work together to find the money. Suddenly Herman is found dead. Meanwhile Mr. Bartholomew calls Regina with some shocking news: Carson Dyle had no brother. As usual Peter/Alex has an explanation. He confesses that he came from a poor family and that he is a thief. His real name is Adam Canfield, but he is keeping the assumed name because the three men really believe he is Dyle's brother. Soon after this confession of Adam's, Gideon becomes the next victim.

Once again Regina and Adam search Charles's carry-on bag for a clue. They discover that the agenda book is missing. Regina remembers that the last appointment was Thursday at 5:00 at the park in the Champs-Élysées. The park is filled with children, rides, and stamp collecting booths. Suddenly everyone realizes that it is the stamps on Charles's letter to Regina that are worth $250,000! Tex is the first one to get back to the hotel. The stamps, however, are not there. Little Jean Louis has taken them. Meanwhile Tex becomes the next victim. He scrawls the word *Dyle* before he dies, so Regina now is forced to believe that Adam is really Dyle and that he is the murderer. Once again she calls Mr. Bartholomew for advice. He tells her to meet him and bring the stamps. Adam chases after her.

In the chaos that follows it is discovered that Mr. Bartholomew is really Carson Dyle, who hadn't died during the German attack. The other three men had left him for dead because he had been shot five times. It is he who kills off the others one by one—not just to get the money, but also to get revenge for their having left him there to die. And the true identity of Peter/Alex/Adam is also revealed. He is Bryan Crookshank, of the U.S. Treasury Department. He has been trying to solve the case of the stolen $250,000 for a long time.

Notes

- Notice the beautiful European settings. From the Swiss Alps to the Champs-Elysées the background scenery ironically adds sophistication and beauty to the violent twisting of the plot.

- *Halliwell's Film and Video Guide* refers to *Charade* as both a "black romantic comedy" and a "macabre [deadly, horrible] farce" (Halliwell 1987, 183). As romantic comedy it fits the definition by way of its two sophisticated, nontraditional, upper-crust main characters. But it is black because the adventures of this romantic pair concern revenge, greed, violence, and murder. A *farce* is, by definition, a play in which the plot depends upon a carefully developed situation rather than on well-developed characters. It is usually a comedy, but the word also means "sham" [something false]. In this case the situation is truly a deadly one, and the plot, which is twisted and deceptive [tricky], is the most important element of the film, as is true of all suspense thrillers. Pauline Kael categorized the film similarly to Halliwell, calling it a "debonair [charming] macabre thriller—romantic, scary, satisfying" (Kael 1991, 130).

- One aspect of the suspense/thriller is the sometimes unrealistic nature of the plot. *Charade* is more faithful to reality than most later films of this genre, but the scene in which Reggie, in a designer suit and high heels, is able to outrun Cary Grant's nimble character certainly stretches credibility. Another point that approaches the unbelievable is the fact that the three men—Herman, Gideon, and Tex—all accept apparently unquestioningly the fact that Cary Grant's character is Carson Dyle's brother. There is at least one other point at which the audience must suspend disbelief. Mr. Bartholomew tells Reggie to cooperate with the CIA by finding out all that she can about the four men and the missing money. In a real spy situation, an average American citizen would most likely be placed immediately out of danger in some sort of protection program rather than told to do her own sleuthing [investigating].

- Typical of any good suspense film are the number and complexity of the red herrings, or false clues. Cary Grant's ever changing character provides many such false clues, as does Carson Dyle's impersonation of a government agent named Bartholomew.

- Atypical of the later suspense/thrillers, *Charade* does not reflect the difficulties of modern society. It is more of an escape fantasy.

- The question is what became of the original $250,000 that Charles recovered from its hiding place. It seems that the three stamps were purchased with the $250,000 that Charles had acquired by selling the furniture and complete contents of his and Reggie's apartment. Reggie tells the police inspector that her husband had no job and that she has no idea where his funds came from. Apparently Charles has been running from his three cohorts for as many as twenty years, living off of the money he dug up and, perhaps, investing it wisely over time. The audience must assume all of this because there are very few clues.

- When first released in 1963, *Charade* was not popular with the media. Critics thought it was too strange a mix of comedy and violence.

- Ms. Hepburn's ultra-high fashion wardrobe [clothing] was provided by the famous French designer Givenchy, a personal friend of hers.

Theme

The film seems to be conveying a message about trust. Regina wanted a divorce from Charles because she was tired of his lies and secrets. Ironically she falls in love with another chronic [habitual] liar. It seems odd that with each new identity and new set of lies he tells her, she still loves him. Perhaps love is a transforming power. "Peter" goes through a gradual transformation into, finally, a perfectly acceptable honest citizen who works for the government. The question is whether Regina contributed to this change. In any case there is still a certain irony in the end: Bryan's last name is Crookshank. A crook is a thief. His character has been transformed, but not erased.

Previewing Questions
D.O.A.

1. The body count is high in this thriller. How many victims are there and in what order are they killed?
2. What does *D.O.A.* mean? Who is D.O.A. in this film?
3. Review the section "Film Noir as Genre" in chapter 2. How is *D.O.A.* a good example of a modern film noir?

D.O.A.

(1988) dirs. Rocky Morton, Annabel Jankel 98 min.
Starring: Dennis Quaid, Meg Ryan

Setting: Christmastime, Texas, during a heat wave

Characters

Dex Cornell [Dennis Quaid]—a well-known author of four books (two of which were bestsellers) and an English professor at a prestigious private university. He and his wife Gail are getting divorced because she claims that he has stopped caring about love and life. Professionally Dex is not happy because he has writer's block: for the past four years he hasn't been able to think of any new material for a novel.

Sydney Fuller [Meg Ryan]—a student in Cornell's English class. She has a crush on him.

Nick Lang [Rob Knepper]—another of Dex's students. He is a computer genius and a potential author.

Plot

The plot begins in flashback, with Dex Cornell recounting to the police what has happened to him during the past thirty-six hours. Death and violence are integral parts of the story. The first victim is Nick Lang, perhaps the brightest [most intelligent] and most capable of Dex's students. He is a scholarship student who entered school through a set of special circumstances. The son of a thief, Nick's father had broken into the mansion of a well-known, wealthy family four years previously and had been killed in a struggle with the owner of the home, Mr. Fitzwaring, who had also been killed. Interestingly, the widow Fitzwaring, feeling pity for the son of the murderous thief, had decided to pay Nick's college tuition. Nick writes a novel for Dex's class and is very anxious for the professor to read it. However, Dex doesn't bother, and Nick suddenly ends up dead, an apparent suicide.

The second murder victim is Gail, Dex's wife. The police think Dex knew about her affair with Nick because, they hypothesize [guess], he found some love letters. The police believe this because they find ashes in the fireplace, which leads them to think Dex burned the love letters there and killed Nick out of jealousy. The police further assume that after her husband had killed Nick, Gail had poisoned Dex in order to get revenge for her lover Nick's death. They conclude, then, that one possible scenario is that Dex killed Gail after she had poisoned him. Another theory the police have is that Nick poisoned Dex and that Dex killed Nick when he found out that he had been poisoned. Yet another theory the police have is that both Nick and Gail poisoned Dex so that he would die and they could be together. The police try to arrest Dex but he escapes, hoping to find, before he dies, the person who poisoned him.

After a bit of investigation, Dex develops his own theories about the deaths of Gail and Nick. He meets Cookie Fitzwaring, daughter of the generous widow Fitzwaring, at a bar on the evening of the day of Nick's murder. Discovering later that she, like his wife, had been in love with Nick, Dex begins to suspect that Cookie's mother had been jealous of her daughter's relationship with Nick and had broken up the relationship because she was also in love with Nick. He theorizes that the widow killed his wife Gail out of jealousy and then killed Nick because she (the widow) couldn't have Nick for herself. When Dex Cornell shows up at the widow's house to accuse her of Nick's and Gail's murder, the chauffeur, Bernard, is ordered to kill him. Cookie suddenly arrives at home and finds that Dex is a prisoner. While attempting to help him escape from Bernard, Cookie accidentally becomes the next murder victim.

In self-defense Dex kills Bernard and then returns to the widow's house to find out from her why she had ordered that he and Nick be killed. She has shocking news that ruins Dex's theory about her being in love with Nick. It seems that Nick was in fact her son and that the thief who had broken into her home four years ago was really her husband, whom she had abandoned twenty years before. The two men, her first husband and Fitzwaring, didn't kill each other, as the police thought. Instead it was the widow Fitzwaring herself who shot both men in order to protect the reputation of her children, Nick and Cookie. And of course she had broken up the romance between Nick and Cookie because she didn't want Cookie to marry Nick, her half-brother. With the heavy realization that they are all dead, she commits suicide.

All his theories wrong, Dex starts again to find his murderer. Figuring that he was poisoned sometime the night before, Dex decides to retrace his steps and go to all the places he had drunkenly visited that night. His student Sydney had been with him, so he enlists her aid, mostly against her will. Eventually he discovers who poisoned him and kills that person. Nevertheless, the poison inside him will soon lead to his death, and as the flashback ends and the color film becomes black and white again, we see the dying Dex sitting in the police station and we know he is a dead man.

Notes

- The opening and closing scenes are in black and white, indicating the bleak [hopeless] reality. The events of the past thirty-six hours, which Cornell is recounting to the police, are all in color. The title sums up

Dex's condition: *D.O.A.* is a police/medical term for Dead On Arrival. By the time he arrives at the police station, he is almost dead. Beyond that fact, on a philosophical level, Dex himself admits that he has been dead inside for the past four years. Upon his arrival at this truth, he is near death. Yet he is saved by having learned, once more, to know the joys of living and the value of life.

- The audience is invited to feel the sensations of the dying main character through the tricks of the camera. The visual vertigo [seasickness] is strong and helps us identify with Dex's dilemma.

- As is typical in suspense films, there are a number of red herrings in the plot. For instance, the theories the police have about who murdered Gail and Nick are not right. Further, Dex's theory about the widow Fitzwaring is also incorrect, as is his assumption that the person who tried to murder him and Sydney in the theatre was Bernard.

- As in Hitchcock's *Notorious*, the emphasis is on drinking and its negative effects. The camera focuses often on the many liquids that Dex imbibes over the course of thirty-six hours.

- In the academic world, professors work toward job security in a process that ends with tenure, which is basically a promise to be installed at that institution until retirement. After being at a university for five or six years, teaching skills and scholarly work are reviewed by a committee. Typically the number of quality articles and books published is the major determiner of whether or not tenure is granted, hence the expression, "Publish or perish [die]." When tenure is assured, promotion in rank and thus salary is possible. The first step is that of assistant professor, then associate professor, and finally full professor.

- This story of a man dying of slow-acting poison and attempting subsequently to find his murderer has been told at least three times: *D.O.A.* (1949), *Color Me Dead* (1969), and now *D.O.A.* (1988). All three versions are certainly candidates for classification not only as thrillers but as dark thrillers, or film noir, like *Laura* [chapter 2]. Like the original version, the 1988 film is "a prime example of a thriller accentuated [emphasized] by factors of cynicism, alienation, chaos, and the corrupt nature of society to convey a dark vision of contemporary America" (Silver and Ward 1992, 77), and in this case, is a dark vision of the academic world, as well.

Theme

- The film's main purpose appears to be to parody [make fun of] academic life. Look what happens, it is saying, when you don't take students and their homework seriously. And the old saying "Publish or perish" is given a real sense of meaning as many people perish in order that one man may keep his job and get promoted. Additionally, Dex represents the weak, impotent [powerless], professorial type at the beginning of the film, but as he becomes a man of action and basically renounces [gives up] his scholarly position, his value as a human being increases and his sex drive returns.

- From a psychological perspective, Dex's problem of writer's block could possibly be related to impotence [the inability of the male to get an erection]. Perhaps one message of the film is that to be very creative (like Nick), a person must also be sexually hungry and active, both physically and intellectually. Because this film is a murder mystery and thriller, there is less emphasis on the development of character, but there appear to be enough clues to suggest that Dex suffers from sexual dysfunction (Geduld 1988, 43).

Previewing Questions
Traces of Red

1. What does the color red suggest to you?
2. The plot twists in this thriller can be confusing. The chances are you may change your mind about the identity of the killer several times. Pay careful attention to all clues: which ones are red herrings?
3. What similarities do you see between this film and *D.O.A*?

Traces of Red

(1992)   dir. Andy Wolk   105 min.
Starring: James Belushi, Lorraine Bracco, Tony Goldwyn, William Russ

Setting: Palm Beach, Florida

Characters

Jack Dobson [James Belushi]—a homocide detective. He has a brother Michael who is a politician. His father was a trumpet player whom he didn't know well. His mother is in a near-vegetative state. Unmarried, he is a "stud" [playboy] who enjoys his role as tough-guy cop.

Michael Dobson [William Russ]—Jack's older, married brother, and a candidate for the state senate.

Steve Frayn [Tony Goldwyn]—Jack's partner at work and his good friend as well. Steve has a wife, Beth, and a little girl, Nancy. Beth is often frustrated by her husband's strange working hours and his inability to spend time with his family.

Ellen Schofield [Lorraine Bracco]—the girlfriend of Jack. Recently widowed, she had been married to a very wealthy man who taught her the social graces and transformed her into a society lady. She had previously been a flight attendant.

Plot

As is the case in many film noir movies, *Traces of Red* has a narrator. The main character recounts for us the events leading up to his apparent death.

The action begins at a dinner party at a fancy restaurant. After the dinner, Jack leaves his date, Ellen, and picks up a waitress, Morgan, taking her home for a night of fun.

The next day, just before a court appearance, he receives an anonymous letter, sealed with a red kiss. It reads "A dead whore [prostitute] is nothing new. Go to court and you'll die too." Jack has to be in court in order to testify against a man named Tony Gareedy, who runs a high-class escort [prostitution] service. Jack had seen Tony in the hotel where a woman, Kimberly Davis, was murdered. Jack is convinced that Tony murdered her. While he is testifying, someone trashes [ruins] his car. Jack believes it was Tony's fat brother, Minnesota, who did it.

On the following day another anonymous letter arrives, stating "You only do it to hurt me more. Live by your lies. Die by my cord." That night Morgan Cassidy, the waitress, is murdered, a cord wrapped around her neck and lipstick smeared on her lips. Found in her room by the police is a poster from a nightclub signed "Love, Russ." The police laboratory analysis finds that the lipstick was Yves St. Laurent's Ruby Red. The lab also discovers that the notes to Jack were made on a printer on which the letters "D" and "L" do not strike properly and that the lipstick on the notes to Jack is Yves St. Laurent Ruby Red. It is a common color. Ellen Schofield uses it and so does Beth, Steve's wife.

Ellen becomes a suspect. During a fund-raising party held at her home to raise money for Michael's senate campaign, Ellen's computer printer is checked for a match to the anonymous notes. It isn't the one, so Jack and Steve arrange to secretly check her printer at work. It doesn't match either.

Meanwhile the third note arrives with this little verse: "Now you know how much it hurts. Prepare to die for Gloria Wertz." Jack explains to Steve that Gloria Wertz was his first-grade teacher. Jack had testified against her in court, claiming that she sexually molested him, putting red lipstick on him and then touching him. A brief investigation leads them to discover that she is dead, but that her son Steven is living in Key West. Steve is sent down to check him out. Ellen surprises him there, for her own reasons. Steve finds out that Steven died of AIDS the year before.

Eventually it becomes clear that Kimberly Davis and Morgan Cassidy were killed by the same person. Jack makes this hypothesis based on the following information: (*a*) both victims were young and attractive; (*b*) both victims' clothes had disappeared after their murder; (*c*) both were wearing Yves St. Laurent Ruby Red lipstick; and (*d*) both victims were mentioned in the anonymous letters Jack had been receiving.

When Steve finds out that both Jack and his brother Michael had been in the hotel the night Kimberly was murdered, he begins to suspect Jack. Meanwhile Beth calls Steve to come home. She then accuses him of having an affair with Ellen. She shows him some clothes that she had found hidden in the garage. He recognizes them as the clothes worn by Morgan Cassidy and Kimberly Davis at the time of their murders. Upon driving to Ellen's house, Steve finds that she, too, has been murdered. Just as he is about to call the police, he sees a car drive away, so he follows it. The car stops at Michael's house. When Steve confronts Michael with Ellen's murder, about which he claims to know nothing, Michael reveals the awful truth: It wasn't Gloria Wertz who molested Jack; it was his own mother. To save the family from embarrassment, a scapegoat [person to blame] had been used—Gloria Wertz. Now it seems clear that Jack is the murderer, driven to crime by his sordid [unclean] past. When Michael and Steve rifle through Jack's things at Jack's apartment, they discover murder weapons and another letter. This time the letter is addressed to Steve and says that Jack really wanted to be caught.

Michael and Steve rush to Jack's little house in the woods, where Jack had taken Beth to be certain of her safety. There Steve shoots Jack. This is the point at which the narrative began. It seems the story has come full circle, but in fact the story isn't over yet . . .

Notes

- Michael's killing of the women he was attracted to reflects his inability to kill the real offender: his mother. Further, the fact that he is attracted to the same women whom Jack has slept with is another reflection on the psychosis caused by the abuse. The mother abused both boys sexually, so in his warped [twisted] and jealous mind, Michael must therefore have the same women Jack had. And he must punish them for their sexuality.

- There are quite a few similarities between the two suspense thrillers *D.O.A.* and *Traces of Red*. Both stories are told in flashback and both have as their narrator the main character. Murder and violence keep the action fast paced and suspense filled. Sex scenes in both films meet Hollywood's criteria for the modern thriller movie. Incest is a problem in both films: Cookie and Nick in *D.O.A.*, Michael, Jack, and their mother in *Traces of Red*. Jealousy contributes to the plots of both films. In *D.O.A.* Hal is jealous of Dex's success and Dex is jealous of Nick's creative talent; in *Traces of Red* Michael is jealous of Jack's playboy/cop image. There are male buddies in both: Hal and Dex in *D.O.A.*, Jack and Steve in *Traces of Red*. Suicide claims lives in both. Mrs. Fitzwaring of *D.O.A.* kills herself because her entire family has been destroyed, and Michael commits suicide in *Traces of Red* because his political reputation is ruined. There are also exciting chase scenes, in cars and on foot, adding to the suspense.

- As in *D.O.A.* and *Charade* there are red herrings. Tony Gareedy is an early suspect. Then Ellen is the prime suspect for a while. For a time we doubt Steve, and later Jack. We even suspect Beth for a short time as she fondles a kitchen knife while in a brooding mood. The Nightwing perfume is also a red herring. One false clue acts as foreshadowing: Steve's little girl plays dead, a scarf wrapped around her neck like a murder weapon and her face smeared with red lipstick. Like her, Jack plays dead in order to catch the real killer.

- One major filmgoers' criticism is that the audience is never made aware of the plan that Jack and Steve have formulated to catch Michael. There are few hints of it. Only after Steve calls Jack from Michael's house do we have some idea that they have set a trap, and we don't know for whom, especially since the next scene is of Michael and Jack discovering incriminating evidence in Jack's apartment.

Themes

- Sexual molestation of young children, particularly by family members, is an insidious crime that leaves emotional and psychological scars [marks] on its victims for life. We get the impression also from this film that Jack and Michael did not have a happy home life. Not only were they abused by their mother but they also had an absent father. Thus the film is also taking the position that an abnormal family life can contribute to psychotic behavior.

- A disturbing motif in this film is the attitude toward women, who are victims and sex objects—"whores." As wives they are neglected, as Beth is, and cheated on, as are Beth and Michael's wife. As sex objects they are used and then killed. Women thus appear to be powerless.

- The negative power of jealousy is made clear through Michael's need to have sex with the same women Jack had. This emotional negative of jealousy is contrasted with the very positive value of trust. Ultimately, throughout their problems, Jack and Steve maintain their trust in and respect for each other. This bond ultimately allows them to solve the murder.

Previewing Questions
Cape Fear

1. This film, like *Psycho*, is a psychological thriller. The antagonist is deeply disturbed. In fact, many of the characters have deep-seated psychological problems. What are they?
2. Also as in *Psycho*, there is a strong emphasis on family. How does this emphasis relate to the theme?
3. As with *D.O.A.* and *Traces of Red*, we are expected to suspend disbelief as more and more unbelievable action occurs on the screen. What are some of the more far-fetched, incredible scenes?

Cape Fear

(1991) dir. Martin Scorsese   128 min.
Starring: Robert De Niro, Nick Nolte, Jessica Lange

Setting: New Essex, North Carolina. Cape Fear is a North Carolina river where the family goes for vacation.

Characters

Max Cady [Robert De Niro]—a Pentecostal [fundamentalist Christian] psychopath with religious tattoos and Bible verses all over his body who has just spent the last fourteen years in prison, serving time for having raped a sixteen-year-old.

Sam Bowden [Nick Nolte]—the criminal lawyer who defended Max Cady fourteen years before but who had actually "buried" [hid] certain evidence that could have kept Cady out of prison.

Leigh Bowden [Jessica Lange]—Sam's wife and a commercial artist.

Danny (Danielle) [Juliette Lewis]—Sam and Leigh's fifteen-year-old daughter. She is a troubled adolescent recently punished at school for smoking pot [marijuana].

Plot

Max Cady is released from prison after fourteen years. He blames Sam Bowden for his lengthy imprisonment. Sam defended Max, but he withheld certain information that could have cleared him. He thought Cady was a menace [risk] to society and that he should definitely be in prison. Cady begins following the Bowden family. Sam tries to buy him off [to convince him with money to stop bothering his family]. Max Cady, however, has lost his wife and daughter, his job, and his self-respect. In fact, he is convinced that it is Sam's fault that it happened.

One upsetting episode after another occurs as Cady stalks [follows] and manipulates the family into a state of panic. When the family dog is poisoned, Sam goes to the police, who can't prove that Cady has broken any laws, so they just decide to watch him closely and to harass [bother] him so that he will leave town. Meanwhile, the stress is building. As the tension and anxiety grow about Cady's behavior, we see more and more closely the imperfections in the Bowden family. For instance, we learn that the family had moved from Georgia to North Carolina in an attempt to start over again after Sam had been unfaithful and Leigh had consequently suffered a bout of depression. And we know that Danny has been experimenting with drugs and has had behavioral problems.

Meanwhile Cady's psychological harassment gets physical: he finds the woman (Lori Davis) whom he thinks Sam is having an affair with and rapes and assaults her. Although the police know Cady's car was at the scene of the crime, the woman who was attacked, Lori, refuses to testify against Cady. She is a legal assistant and doesn't want to be questioned about rape and be humiliated in front of all the people she works with. Besides, in love with Sam, she wants to protect him and his reputation.

After this horrible violence against his friend Lori, Sam decides to hire a private detective because the police still can't help. The detective is supposed to follow Cady and get more information about him and his habits. The detective tries to convince Sam to employ some thugs [tough men] to beat Cady up and scare him out of town. Meanwhile, Cady calls Danny and pretends to be her drama teacher, telling her to meet for class in the theatre at school. He's very charming and particularly likes young girls. After all, he was in prison for raping a sixteen-year-old. He understands the troubles of adolescents—their anger at their parents and their attempts to become adults. After Cady approaches Danny, Sam is so angry that he agrees with the private detective that some men should beat Cady up. The plan backfires and Cady beats the thugs up instead. At this point Cady is even more determined not to give up until he has gotten his revenge on Sam and his family.

Cady takes Sam to court for having hired someone to beat him up. Sam almost loses his license to practice law because of that and because Cady also tells his lawyer about the evidence that Sam had buried during Cady's trial fouteen years ago. Now Sam is desperate. He asks the detective to get him a gun to carry. Sam has to go to a special hearing to find out if he will be disbarred [lose his privileges to practice law] because of what he did to Max Cady. Sam pretends to get on the plane to Raleigh for this special meeting, but in fact he comes back with his family. It is a kind of trap. The detective is at home with the family, ready to catch and kill Cady if he tries to enter the house. But somehow Cady gets in, kills the maid, impersonates her, and kills the detective. The family manage to escape, and they decide to hide on a houseboat on the coast, at Cape Fear. Unfortunately for them, Cady has attached himself to the undercarriage of the car. After the family get established on the boat, Cady shows up and begins to terrorize them. What he wants is revenge. He wants Sam to feel the same kind of loss that he felt, so he tortures everyone. What happens in the end, Cady's death, is predictable. He expected to get his revenge and then to die.

Notes

- The title, *Cape Fear*, has two meanings. Fear is the weapon Cady uses to manipulate the family. Cape Fear is the place where the climax and resolution of the conflict occur.

- The system that put Cady in jail also gave him the ability to beat the system. He learned to read while in prison, and most of the time he read law books, which taught him how to avoid getting caught and how to manipulate the law to his own advantage.

- Like Hitchcock and Wilder, Scorsese can be considered an auteur. As a director he has made many films, but one kind seems to be his favorite. He likes suspense/thrillers in which the common person, or especially the average American family, is harassed and tortured by criminals. He enjoys incorporating violence into his films, too (Kauffmann 1991, 29). Furthermore, Scorsese appears to be fascinated by obsessive personalities like Max Cady. Many of his protagonists are obsessed, sometimes for the good of society and sometimes not: *Mean Streets*, *Taxi Driver*, *Raging Bull*, *The Last Temptation of Christ*, and "Life Lessons" from the film *New York Stories* (Alleva 1991, 748–49). By definition, another characteristic of the auteur is the repetitious use of actors or characters. Robert De Niro has appeared in seven Scorsese films (Corliss 1991, 84).

- As an auteur, Scorsese is naturally concerned about innovative [new] camera techniques and ways to move the plot forward. In *Cape Fear* he uses several. For instance, he starts a few scenes with a loud sound, perhaps in an attempt to frighten the audience into readiness for the next event. At times he uses a red filter on the camera lens to suggest blood, just as at other times he employs X-ray images to suggest hidden fears that may become real. And there is the heavy, unlyrical [not melodic] music of Elmer Bernstein, who is imitating the original score [music] by Bernard Herrmann (Hitchcock's favorite) of the 1962 version of *Cape Fear* (Kauffmann 1991, 28–29). Scorsese also employs the extreme close-up much more frequently than is common. In this case such shots are limited in their focus to one character, Sam Bowden. We can assume that this is because we are supposed to be constantly aware that the family is in jeopardy [at risk] as a direct result of his own wrongdoings, and we are to share his grief, anger, and frustration as he attempts to make things right again.

- Robert Mitchum and Gregory Peck were the main characters in the 1962 version of this film. Mitchum played the menacing ex-convict to Peck's much more innocent lawyer. They have minor roles in this 1991 version, as does Martin Balsam, who also figured prominently in the original. The idea for the story itself came from a novel, *The Executioners*, by John D. MacDonald (Alleva 1991, 748).

- As is true with most movies of the thriller genre, the antagonist, Max Cady, is almost superhuman. Realism is lost when time after time Cady is hurt but unstopped. The three thugs beat him severely, but he overwhelms them. Danny throws boiling water in his face and later sets him on fire. Sam beats him and throws him overboard, yet it takes a hurricane, handcuffs, and a sinking boat to kill Cady. Besides his physical strength, he also has read law and is well versed in literary fiction (Alleva 1991, 749). It is a tribute to the strength of the formula of the thriller genre that the audience never suspends belief.

Themes

- As in other films of the suspense/thriller genre such as *Psycho*, *Psycho IV*, and *Fatal Attraction*, the family is the main focus. Either the family is dysfunctional [abnormal] or it is divided by outside forces, or both. The message seems to be that the cornerstone of civilization is the family and that when the family disintegrates [falls apart] or is ruptured [broken], society breaks down and there is violence, chaos, and insanity. Interestingly, the family unit was not a strong one even before Cady came along. Sam Bowden is a successful, semi-honest lawyer who has been unfaithful to the law and to his wife. Leigh Bowden seems to feel contempt for her husband; consequently, they spend a lot of time screaming at each other. No doubt the young daughter's problems are complicated by her parents' animosity toward each other (Alleva 1991, 749). The trauma that Max Cady brings to their lives is, ironically, what pulls the family together.

- Another significant theme seems to be the importance of ethics. Sam withheld information in court that could have prevented Cady's going to jail. While it is true that Cady was a bad man, a psychopath, the point is that the legal system is also a cornerstone of civilization, and when laws are broken, the system and society break down. Max Cady is the symbol of this breakdown of society. Notice, too, that to emphasize this point, every time Sam breaks the law (for example, having Cady beaten up, and leaving his house rather than waiting for the police after the detective and maid are murdered), things go badly for him

(Sam). The final scenes of the raging water, the houseboat loose and unpiloted (and finally destroyed), the violence inside the boat—all of this is symbolic of the breakdown of society.

- Interestingly, the information Sam Bowden withheld in Cady's case concerned the rape victim's character. She was considered promiscuous [easy with sexual favors]. In the Georgia courtroom, Sam thought, such evidence would most likely have freed Cady on the grounds that the girl had been asking for trouble and did not deserve respect. Understated and subtle, one subtheme of this film may be the idea that rape is never acceptable or forgivable, no matter what the character of the victim.

- In connection with these themes is the idea that the perversion of religion for purposes of revenge also contributes to the breakdown of religion, and a godless society is a society in chaos. Cady feels as if he has been crucified. He sees himself as a Christ-figure, having been put in jail unjustly.

Additional Film Units for Consideration

Sex Roles in American Comedic Film—Some Like It Hot (1959), *Tootsie* (1982), *Victor/Victoria* (1982), *Mrs. Doubtfire* (1993). In these movies, cross-dressing, or transvestism, is employed as a means to an end; i.e. each cross-dressing main character is forced by circumstances to undergo role reversal. In every case this change is beneficial to the character. In addition, the issue of homosexuality as an alternative lifestyle is embraced or accepted to some degree in each film. Examining transvestism and homosexuality makes for lively film study.

Westerns: The Death of the Old West—Shane (1953), *Will Penny* (1968), *The Shootist* (1976), *The Cowboys* (1972). These films illustrate the demise of the Old West—the lawless, Indian-infested, buffalo-filled plains where cowboys were king. Early westerns glorified this heroic individualist and loner, but later civilization—in the form of sheriffs, churches, towns, and most importantly, the railroad and wives—usurped the cowboy's place. Now Hollywood is busy with revisionist westerns that are meant to realign our sympathies and focus on the atrocities committed by cowboys on the Indians (*Dances With Wolves* 1990), and to open our eyes to the useless romanticism of the myth of the Old West (Eastwood's *The Unforgiven* 1992).

Parodies: A Special Brand of Comedy—Blazing Saddles (1974) parodies the western, *Airplane* (1980) rips disaster movies of the 1970s, *Spaceballs* (1987) parodies Lucas's *Star Wars* pictures, *Dead Men Don't Wear Plaid* (1982) pokes fun at the film noir/Sam Spade detective stories, *Monster Squad* (1987) parodies the horror film, *Heathers* (1989) stabs teen pix, and *High Anxiety* (1977) is a Hitchcock spoof. Parodies are usually a great source for idiomatic speech/vocabulary items.

Populist Films: A Slice of American History—Mr. Deeds Goes to Town (1936), *Mr. Smith Goes To Washington* (1939), *The Grapes of Wrath* (1940). These films focus poignantly on the social problems of their era as well as making very clear the American values of the 1930s.

Remakes: Hollywood Does It Again—Here Comes Mr. Jordan (1941) became *Heaven Can Wait* (1978), *Father of the Bride* (1950/1991), *Cape Fear* (1962/1991), *A Star Is Born* (1937/1954/1976), *Born Yesterday* (1951/1993), *The Postman Always*

Rings Twice (1946/1981). These films make great fodder for comparison papers and also allow the students to see how fashion, values, acting styles, dialogue, and such have changed over time.

Film Noir—*Double Indemnity* (1944), *The Big Sleep* (1946), *Sorry Wrong Number* (1948), *The Asphalt Jungle* (1950), *Sunset Boulevard* (1950), *Strangers on a Train* (1951), *The Big Heat* (1953). This genre sprang from the gloomy war days of 1939 and onward into the mid-1950s. The dark, serious, pessimistic tone can be off-putting, but these films are a unique part of the American filmstyle and present a coherent picture of urban America in social decay.

Comedy—*The Seven-Year Itch* (1955), *The Frisco Kid* (1979), *A Fish Called Wanda* (1988), *Housesitter* (1992). Comedy usually explores the relationship of its characters to society by either insisting that the characters conform to the social norms by film's end or, more likely, by encouraging the development or furtherance of the main character's antisocial behavior in a way that allows the film to ridicule social norms and bourgeois values. Further, much of what is comic comes from the stereotyping of the characters. In the case of *A Fish Called Wanda*, the film ridicules the stereotypes on both sides of the Atlantic—American and British.

Fairy Tales—*Beauty and the Beast*, *Sleeping Beauty*, *The Tale of the Frog Prince*, *Cinderella*, *Snow White and the Seven Dwarves*, *Little Red Riding Hood*, *The Little Mermaid*, *The Nightingale*, *Aladdin and His Wonderful Lamp*, etc. In 1982 and 1983 Shelley Duvall produced an excellent collection of children's stories called *Faerie Tale Theatre*. Some of Hollywood's best-known personalities appear in these sixty-minute dramas. The list includes Susan Sarandon, Matthew Broderick, Elizabeth McGovern, Vanessa Redgrave, Mick Jagger, and James Earl Jones. Students of all ages enjoy these stories, and the tales lend themselves well to discussions of variations in the story from country to country. A good reference book: *The Hard Facts of the Grimms' Fairy Tales* by Maria Tatar.

Feature-Length Soap Operas—*Dark Victory* (1939), *Back Street* (1941), *Mildred Pierce* (1945), *Imitation of Life* (1959), *Peyton Place* (1957), *Return to Peyton Place* (1961), *The Betsy* (1978), *An Inconvenient Woman* (1991). All these films display certain of the typical elements found in soaps—the socioeconomic contrasts, the "good" versus "bad" characters, risqué topics like incest, abortion, illegitimacy, a focus on the dark side of humanity, family problems, social problems, and all of it punctuated by melodramatic music and a large cast of characters involved in an intertwining plot.

From Literature to Film: Short Story and Novel Adaptations
Short stories:
    Willa Cather "Paul's Case"
    Kate Chopin "The Story of an Hour"
    William Faulkner "A Rose for Emily," "Dry September"

Additional Film Units for Consideration / 163

F. Scott Fitzgerald "Babylon Revisited"
   (film version: *The Last Time I Saw Paris*)
Mary E. Wilkins Freeman "The Revolt of 'Mother'"
Ernest Hemingway "Soldier's Home"
Sarah Orne Jewett "A White Heron"
James Joyce "The Dead"
James Thurber "The Secret Life of Walter Mitty"
(Some titles may appear in the education section of the video stores.)

Novels and Plays:
Peter Benchley *Jaws*
Thomas Berger *Little Big Man*
Joe David Brown *Addie Pray* (film version: *Paper Moon*)
Truman Capote *Breakfast at Tiffany's*
Vera Caspary *Laura*
Michael Crichton *The Andromeda Strain, Jurassic Park, Rising Sun*
Phillip Dick *Do Androids Dream of Electric Sheep?*
   (film version: *Blade Runner*)
Jack Finney *The Body Snatchers*
   (film version: *The Invasion of the Body Snatchers*)
John Grisham *The Client, The Firm, The Pelican Brief*
Ernest Hemingway *To Have and Have Not, Islands in the Stream*
William Bradford Huie *The Americanization of Emily*
Richard Hooker *M.A.S.H.*
Shirley Jackson *The Haunting of Hill House*
   (film version: *The Haunting*)
James Jones *From Here to Eternity*
Ken Kesey *One Flew Over the Cuckoo's Nest, Sometimes a Great Notion* [*Never
   Give an Inch*]
Harper Lee *To Kill a Mockingbird*
Carson McCullers *The Heart Is A Lonely Hunter, The Member of the Wedding*
Grace Metalious *Peyton Place*
James Michener *Sayonara, Hawaii*
Robert Nathan *Portrait of Jennie*
John O'Hara *Butterfield 8*
Katherine Ann Porter *Ship of Fools*
Ayn Rand *The Fountainhead*
Harold Robbins *The Betsy, The Carpetbaggers*
John Steinbeck *The Grapes of Wrath, East of Eden*
Tennessee Williams *Cat on a Hot Tin Roof, The Glass Menagerie, A Streetcar
   Named Desire*
Richard Wright *Native Son*

Appendix

Where to Find Videos

Call or write for the following catalogs.

Critic's Choice Video
P.O. Box 749
Itasca, IL 60143-0749
(800)367-7765

The Video Catalog
P.O. Box 64267
St. Paul, MN 55164-0428
(800)71VIDEO

Time Warner Viewer's Edge
P.O. Box 3925
Milford, CT 06460
(800)544-1905

VideoYesterYear
Box C
Sandy Hook, CT 06482
(800)243-0987

Movies Unlimited
6736 Castor Avenue
Philadelphia, PA 19149
(800)523-0823

Fusion Video
17311 Fusion Way
Country Club Hills, IL 60478
(800)959-0061

Elliot M. Katt: Bookseller
Books on the Performing Arts
8568 Melrose Ave.
Los Angeles, CA 90069
(800)445-4561

Some Sources of Film Information

Filmfacts
Films in Review
Film Journal
Film Quarterly
Film Review Index
Halliwell's Film and Video Guide
Journal of Film and Video
Literature/Film Quarterly
Magill's Cinema Annual
Motion Picture Guide
New York Times Film Reviews
Screenworld

References

Alleva, Richard. 1991. "Screen: Obsession Overreaches." *Commonweal*, 20 Dec., 748–50.
Ansen, David. 1980. "Get the Boss." *Newsweek*, 22 Dec., 72–73.
Ansen, David, and Martin Kasindorf. 1980. "Supersecretaries." *Newsweek*, 31 Mar., 80–81.
Bell-Metereau, Rebecca. 1985. *Hollywood Androgyny*. New York: Columbia University Press.
Bywater, Tim, and Thomas Sobchack. 1989. *An Introduction to Film Criticism*. New York: Longman.
Chase, Donald. 1994. "My Favorite Year." *Film Comment*, Sept.-Oct., 60–72.
Corliss, Richard. 1988a. "'Bad' Women and Brutal Men." *Time*, 21 Nov., 127.
———. 1988b. "Two Out of Five Ain't Bad." *Time*, 19 Dec., 78–79.
———. 1991. "Filming at Full Throttle." *Time*, 11 Nov., 84–85.
Geduld, Harry. 1988. "The Sweet Smell of Failure." *Humanist*, July/Aug., 43.
Giannetti, Louis. 1982. *Understanding Movies*. 3d ed. New Jersey: Prentice-Hall.
Glicksman, Marlaine. 1989. "Spike Lee's Bed-Stuy BBQ." *Film Comment*, July/Aug., 12–18.
Halliwell, Leslie. 1987. *Halliwell's Film and Video Guide*. 6th ed. New York: Charles Scribner's Sons.
Harvey, James. 1987. *Romantic Comedy in Hollywood, from Lubitsch to Sturges*. New York: Alfred A. Knopf.
Haskell, Molly. 1974. *From Reverence to Rape: The Treatment of Women in the Movies*. New York: Penguin Books.
Jameson, Richard T., ed. 1994. *They Went Thataway*. San Francisco: Mercury House.
Jasper, Jann. 1992. "Rape: Are You At Risk?" *New Woman*, Dec., 80–86.
Kael, Pauline. 1984. *Taking It All In*. New York: Holt, Rinehart, and Winston.
———. 1991. *5001 Nights at the Movies*. New York: Henry Holt and Co.
Katz, Ephraim. 1979. *The Film Encyclopedia*. New York: Perigee Books.
Kauffmann, Stanley. 1988. "Double Meaning." *New Republic*, 21 Nov., 30–31.
———. 1991. "Southern Discomfort." *New Republic*, 9 Dec., 28–29.
Keough, Peter. 1994. "On Women, Films, and the Women's Film." In *They Went Thataway*, edited by Richard T. Jameson, 279–83. San Francisco: Mercury House.
Klawans, Stuart. 1989. "Films." *Nation*, 17 July, 98–101.
Knight, Arthur. 1957. *The Liveliest Art*. New York: New American Library.

Konigsberg, Ira. 1987. *The Complete ILM Dictionary*. New York: New American Library.

McClure, Arthur, ed. 1971. *The Movies: An American Idiom*. Rutherford: Fairleigh Dickinson University Press.

Madsen, Axel. 1969. *Billy Wilder*. Bloomington: Indiana University Press.

Naremore, James. 1973. *Filmguide to Psycho*. Bloomington: Indiana University Press.

Rainer, Peter. 1994. "On Psychonoir." In *They Went Thataway*, edited by Richard T. Jameson, 26–30. San Francisco: Mercury House.

Samuels, Charles Thomas. 1972. *Encountering Directors*. New York: DaCapo Press.

Scheuer, Steven. 1985. *Movies on TV 1986–1987*. 11th ed. Toronto: Bantam Books.

Schickel, Richard. 1991. "Gender Bender." *Time*, 24 June, 52–56.

Selby, Spencer. 1984. *Dark City: The Film Noir*. Jefferson, N.C.: Farland.

Sennett, Ted. 1992. *Laughing In The Dark: Movie Comedy from Groucho to Woody*. New York: St. Martin's.

Silver, Alain, and Elizabeth Ward, eds. 1992. *Film Noir*. 3d ed. Woodstock, New York: Overlook Press.

Sinyard, Neil. 1986. *The Films of Alfred Hitchcock*. New York: Gallery Books.

Spoto, Donald. 1992. *The Art of Alfred Hitchcock*. 2d ed. New York: Anchor Books.

Sragow, Michael. 1994. "Alfred Hitchcock: *Rear Window*." In *They Went Thataway*, edited by Richard T. Jameson, 150–54. San Francisco: Mercury House.

Telotte, J. P. 1989. *Voices in the Dark*. Urbana and Champaign: University of Illinois Press.

Thomas, John. 1972. "Gobble, Gobble . . . One of Us!" In *Focus on the Horror Film*, edited by Roy Huss and T. J. Ross, 135–39. New Jersey: Prentice-Hall.

Tompkins, Jane. 1992. *West of Everything: The Inner Life of Westerns*. New York: Oxford University Press.

Tudor, Andrew. 1991. *Monsters and Mad Scientists*. 1989. Reprint, Oxford: Blackwell.

Tuska, Jon. 1985. *The American West in Film*. Westport, Conn.: Greenwood Press.

Wolf, Leonard. 1989. *Horror: A Connoisseur's Guide to Literature and Film*. New York: Factson File.

Wood, Robin. 1977. *Hitchcock's Films*. South Brunswick: A. S. Barnes.

———. 1989. *Hitchcock's Films Revisited*. New York: Columbia University Press.

Zinman, David. 1970. *50 Classic Motion Pictures*. New York: Bonanza Books.

Quizzes

King Kong Quiz

1. *King Kong* is about the struggle between good and evil. There are many manifestations of both good and evil. List some of them:

   Good   Evil

2. Why is Ann included on the trip to Skull Island?

3. As "boyfriends," Kong and Jack are similar in their treatment of Ann. Explain.

4. Carl Denham is ruthless. He will do anything to make a picture (and money!). Give several examples of his exploitation [abuse].

   (a)
   (b)
   (c)

5. *King Kong* is filled with symbolism. Give examples.

   Symbol   Interpretation

   (a)
   (b)
   (c)

6. The main characters are flat rather than well developed. Why?

7. In what ways is Kong a sympathetic character?

8. This film was made in 1933. In what ways is it less believable or authentic now?

9. Explain what Denham meant when he uttered those final, famous words: "It was Beauty killed the Beast."

10. What did you like or dislike about this early film classic?

Bonus: How many monsters are killed on Skull Island?

Laura Quiz

1. The film begins with an investigation into a murder. Who is the faceless corpse? How was this person killed? Why was this person the victim of murder?

2-5. Name each suspect and the motive:

    Suspect   *Motive*

  (a)

  (b)

  (c)

  (d)

6. Explain the significance of the following objects:

    (a) the key

    (b) the clock

7. Why did McPherson want everyone to suspect that he believed Laura was the murderer?

8. Many of the characters in this drama are not very likeable ones. Which did you think was the most despicable [meanest]?

9. Why is it acceptable to the audience for Mark McPherson to love Laura but not for Waldo Lydecker or Shelby Carpenter to love her?

10. List some ways in which this film is a good example of the film noir genre.

High Noon Quiz

1. What is the significance of the title of this film?

2. What is the importance of the ballad that we hear throughout the film?

3. Who is Helen Ramirez and why does Will come to see her that day?

4. Why does Amy come to visit Helen Ramirez? From this visit, what do we learn about the character of both women?

5. List some of the reasons why people refuse to help Marshal Cane fight against the badmen.

6. What is the reason for the scenes between Harve and Will?

7. During the shoot-out, how does Marshal Cane escape from the burning barn?

8. Who is the only person who helps Will? Why is this fact so important?

9. Do you think Marshal Cane was right to stay on in town? Why? If he had left, do you think that Frank Miller's gang would have caused trouble anyway for the town?

10. How is this film similar to the westerns you have seen? How is it different?

Some Like It Hot Quiz

1. Why does Spats Columbo kill Toothpick Charlie?

2. Why do Joe and Jerry have to leave Chicago?

3. Consider the characters of Joe and Sugar.

    (a) What are his two biggest weaknesses?

    (b) What is her biggest weakness?

4. Why does Jerry (Daphne) decide to marry Osgood? What is his(her) plan?

5. How do Spats and his gang discover Joe and Jerry in Miami?

6. What happens to Spats and why?

7. Give some examples of the subtle homosexual undertone of the film.

8. In this film transvestism, or cross-dressing, is employed as a means to an end. In other words, Jerry and Joe are forced by circumstances beyond their control to undergo a role reversal. In both Jerry's and Joe's case, the change is a positive one. Explain how.

9. What, in your opinion, is the most outrageous [funniest] line of dialogue in the movie?

10. Which is the funniest scene?

Bonus: Whose accent is Joe imitating when he is wooing Sugar?

Pat and Mike Quiz

1. Why does Pat tell the club pro that her handicap is her beau [boyfriend]?

2. How are the characters of Mike Conovan and Collier Weld different?

3. What are the "Three Big Questions"? Who asks them? How do they change by the end of the film?

4. What kind of business do Mike and his "business associates" have?

5. What does Pat say to Hucko to help him to improve his boxing skills?

6. Why does Mike get angry at Pat for protecting him against his business partners? How does she make him feel good again after that?

7. What is the best indicator of Pat's growing confidence in herself?

8. Who is the best man for Pat? Give three reasons or examples.
    (a)
    (b)
    (c)

9. What did you like best about this film?

10. What did you like the least?

9 to 5 Quiz

1. What are the women's three fantasies and how does each one become a reality?

   (a) fantasy   (a) reality

   (b) fantasy   (b) reality

   (c) fantasy   (c) reality

2. What are the three events that anger Judy, Violet, and Doralee enough for them to refuse to accept their situation anymore?

   (a) Judy:

   (b) Violet:

   (c) Doralee:

3. List five ways in which Mr. Frank Hart is a sexist, egotistical, lying, hypocritical boss.

   (a)
   (b)
   (c)
   (d)
   (e)

4. Describe the process of Judy's liberation.

5. How do the three women plan to blackmail Hart?

6. (a) How does Hart find out about the poisoned coffee?

   (b) Why is it so important to the story that Hart find out about the coffee?

7. List some of the changes (for the better) that the three women cause around the office in Hart's absence.

   (a)
   (b)
   (c)
   (d)

8. What is one of the themes of this film?

Bonus: Who sang the title song for this film?

Working Girl Quiz

1. What prevents Tess from advancing to a higher position in the same manner as others who work in her company?

2. What two events does Tess experience that make her decide to make things happen for herself?

    (a)

    (b)

3. As Katharine's "representative," what sorts of changes in her appearance and behavior does Tess make?

4. What deal does Tess's company make with Trask Industries?

5. Contrast Tess's boyfriend, Mick, with her partner, Jack. Which one is better for her and why?

6. Name two ways in which this film is similar to *9 to 5*.

    (a)

    (b)

7. In what ways is it different?

    (a)

    (b)

8. Compare Katharine Parker (*Working Girl*) to Frank Hart (*9 to 5*).

9. What is the theme of the film?

10. What did you like best about this film?

Thelma and Louise Quiz

1. List four of the big mistakes that the two women make. (What is the first and most tragic one?)

    (a)
    (b)
    (c)
    (d)

2. List the two reasons why Louise shot Harlan.

    (a)
    (b)

3. Why doesn't Louise accept Jimmy's engagement ring and wedding proposal?

4. At what point does Thelma become more responsible and protective of Louise?

5. Why does Louise refuse to travel through Texas to get to Mexico?

6. Why is J. D. an important character in the story?

7. Explain the symbolism of the hats that Thelma and Louise wear.

8. Which of the male characters is the most supportive of Thelma and Louise? Explain your answer.

9. Compare *Thelma and Louise* with another feminist film we have seen.

10. What did you like most and/or least about this film?

Freaks Quiz

1. What is so unusual about the friendship between Venus and Frieda?

2. Why does Cleo want to kill Hans, and how exactly does she plan to do it?

3–5. In his book *The Film Encyclopedia*, Katz writes: "Compassionate as it was for the plight [fate] of its unfortunate characters, the film was tainted [dirtied] with melodramatic excess and [was] exploitative and sensational."

   (a) In what ways was it melodramatic?

   (b) How was it exploitative, that is, how did it use the characters in a negative way?

   (c) Is it still sensational [exciting, shocking]?

6. Did the director intend this film to be

   (a) a serious and sympathetic portrayal of freaks;
   (b) a perverse [contrary, disobedient] kind of comedy; or
   (c) a morality play?

   Explain your choice.

7. What, do you think, is the universal appeal and fascination with circuses and sideshows?

8. Have your views about physically handicapped people been changed by your viewing of this film?

9–10. Do you think that the code of ethics of the freaks is too strict? In other words, did Cleo deserve to be treated as she was? Why did the freaks kill Hercules but only maim [physically change] Cleo? Which is the worse fate? Did Hercules deserve to die?

Forbidden Quiz

1. Explain the multifaceted nature [many meanings] of the title.

2. What are the Nuremberg Laws and how do they apply to this story?

3. What motivates Nina to become involved in helping the Jews?

4. How is interfaith/interracial romance treated in this film? For instance, how is news of Nina's pregnancy received?

5. Why does Fritz come to stay in Nina's home? How does his life there in her apartment symbolize the problem of all the Jews?

6. Why does Nina choose the homosexual to help her? How is his situation mirrored in that of the Jews?

7. What important role does Max play in Fritz's life?

8. Explain the symbolic significance of the baby's death.

9. Explain the supreme irony of the film's conclusion.

10. How are *Freaks* and *Forbidden* thematically linked? Be specific.

The Accused Quiz

1. Who is/are "The Accused"? Why is the title ironic?

2. Sarah's behavior changes in response to the trauma of her rape experience. Describe the changes.

3. The relationship of Katherine and Sarah goes through several stages [steps]. Describe them.

4. Why doesn't Sarah have a good case?

5. Why does Katherine decide to prosecute the witnesses?

6. What is the verdict? What is the significance of such a verdict?

7. Consider this picture from a feminist's point of view. Are there any sympathetic malecharacters? If not, how does this affect the message/theme of the film?

8. Explain the importance of the character of Kenneth Joyce.

9. Do you know of anyone who has been raped? How would/did you react to someone who had suffered such a terrible indignity?

10. How does this film illustrate sexual discrimination?

Do The Right Thing Quiz

1. Describe Da Mayor and Mister Señor Love Daddy. What are they like and how are they important?

2. What part does the weather play?

3. When do the tensions between the races first start?

4. What two events that night cause the riot?

5. Every group has a stereotype, and every group hates another group. Explain, using examples from the film.

6. Did you find Sal to be a sympathetic character? And Mookie? Why or why not?

7. Note the title. In your opinion, did Mookie do the right thing? Explain your answer.

8. Which philosophy do you embrace—that of Martin Luther King, Jr., or that of Malcolm X? Why?

9. Which of the characters of the community did you like best and why?

10. What was, for you, the most compelling [powerful] part of this film?

Bachelor Mother Quiz

1. Why does Freddie Miller think that the father of Polly's baby is David?

2–3. Give two examples of visual humor in this film.

   (a)

   (b)

4. How does the older Merlin contribute to the plot?

5–7. Referring to the section, "Aspects of Romantic Comedy," and your notes for this film, mention three ways in which this film is an example of the classic romantic comedy.

   (a)
   (b)
   (c)

8–9. Give two examples of mistaken identity (a big element in romantic comedy!).

   (a)

   (b)

10. How would this story have been different if Polly really had been the baby's mother?

Bonus: Does David *ever* believe Polly's story that the baby isn't hers?

The Thrill of It All Quiz

1. What's the meaning of the title of the film? The thrill of *what*?

2. How did Mrs. Boyer get the job as the Happy Soap spokeswoman?

3. What's the basic conflict between Dr. and Mrs. Boyer?

4. Why is the character of Mrs. Frawley so important to the theme/message of the film?

5. Why did the first housekeeper quit?

6. Give one example of how this film is similar to the romantic comedy of the 1930s and 1940s.

7. Why did the Boyer family get a swimming pool?

8. When does Beverly decide to give up her job—and why?

9. In what ways is this not like a romantic comedy? Explain how it is more a product of the post–World War Two tradition. (Refer to the section "Aspects of the Romantic Comedy" for more details.)

10. What did you like most about this film?

What's Up, Doc? Quiz

1. Why did Judy pretend she knew "Steve"?

2. Describe the three major characters (in your own words!).

    (a)
    (b)
    (c)

3. Who was the man with the golf clubs?

4. What is the relationship between the house detective and Fritz at the front desk?

5. Describe three whacky [crazy] events that happen during the film.

    (a)
    (b)
    (c)

6–8. Explain at least three ways in which this film is like the classic romantic comedies of the 1930s and 1940s.

    (a)
    (b)
    (c)

9. Who pays for all the damage done by Howard and Judy? Why?

10. What was your favorite scene in this comedy? Why?

Bonus: What was Judy's relationship to the courtroom judge?

Moonstruck Quiz

1. What does the title mean?

2. Give some examples of Italian culture as illustrated in this film.

3. Give three examples of the different kinds of love as shown in this film.

   (a)
   (b)
   (c)

4. Why does Loretta want to marry Johnny?

5. Why does Loretta want to marry Ronny?

6. Why does Loretta's father have an affair? (Why do men chase women?)

7. How does this film compare with the other romantic comedies of this unit? Explain!

8. Which types of love illustrated in this film fit your own personal definition of love?

9. What aspects of the Italian culture shown in this film can also be found in your own culture?

10. How is this film similar to the Cinderella story? Has this Cinderella motif [theme] appeared in other films in this unit?

Notorious Quiz

1. What does the word *notorious* mean? How many of the characters are, in your opinion, notorious? Why?

2. What is the significance of the 1934 wine bottle?

3. What is symbolic about wine and drinking in this film?

4. Why is Alicia the perfect spy for this mission?

5. Consider two of the lead characters, Alicia and Alex.

    (a) Why is Alicia such a sympathetic character?

    (b) Is Alex also a likeable character? Why or why not?

6. Is Dev in love with Alicia? How do you know?

7. The party at Alex's house is given so that Alicia can be introduced as Alex's new wife, but why does Alicia really want him to have the party?

8. How does Alex find out Alicia is a spy?

9. When does Alicia realize she has been poisoned?

10. What is going to happen to Sebastian at the end of the film? Why?

Rear Window Quiz

1. What is the big conflict between Jeff and Lisa?

2. When does Lisa first begin to believe Jeff's story about Thorwald's murdering his wife? What evidence really convinces her?

3. Why is the dog killed? Who kills it?

4. Why does Thorwald kill his wife?

5. Why is Mrs. Thorwald's wedding ring so important as evidence?

6. How does Thorwald know where Jeff lives?

7. The conflict between Lisa and Jeff seems to be resolved by the end of the movie. How do we know this?

8. At film's end, other neighbors' problems also seem to be resolved. Give some examples.

9. The title *Rear Window* has an obvious meaning and a deeper one that concerns the theme. Explain.

10. Do you think it was ethical [morally correct] for Jeff to watch his neighbors and to attempt to interfere with their lives? What would have happened if he hadn't?

Bonus: Do you think that Jeff's other leg is broken because he needs to be punished for his voyeurism?

North by Northwest Quiz

1. Consider the character of Roger O. Thornhill.

    (a) What is he like?

    (b) How has his personality changed by the end of the film?

2. Who is George Kaplan and why is he important to the plot?

3. What two things did Thornhill do that caused Vandamm's agents to think he was Kaplan?

4. Why does Vandamm want Thornhill/Kaplan dead?

5. After the murder at the United Nations, why didn't the CIA people try to help Thornhill?

6. Who is the double agent? What is this agent's function [job]?

7. Twice Eve Kendall saves Thornhill. How?

    (a)
    (b)

8. Who is involved in the love triangle?

9. What is inside the statuette that Vandamm plans to take out of the country?

10. Who was your favorite character in this film and why?

Bonus: Name all of the places Thornhill travels to.

Psycho Quiz

1. How much money does Marion steal, and why?

2. The audience knows that Marion will not escape without being discovered. One reason is that her boss actually sees her driving out of town after she told him she was going to the bank and then home to bed. List some other mistakes she makes.

3. Norman speaks to Marion about "traps."

    (a) What is his trap?

    (b) What is her trap?

4. Notice the striking symbolism in this film.

    (a) What is the symbolic significance of Hitchcock's emphasis on the eyes?

    (b) Describe and explain another recurring symbol in this film.

5. What shocking fact about Norman's past do Sam and Lila find out when they go to see the sheriff of Fairvale?

6. What happens to Arbogast? Why?

7. There are many contrasts in this film. List several of them.

8. Why does Norman dress up in his mother's clothing and murder young, beautiful women? In other words, how does the psychiatrist explain it?

9. What was your favorite scene in this movie? Why?

10. What did you not like about this film?

Charade Quiz

1. (a) What is Regina's husband's name?
   (b) Does she still love him?
   (c) When the police ask her about him and his background, what can she tell them?

2. (a) How does Charles die?
   (b) Where was he going at the time of his murder?
   (c) What did he have with him at the time of his death? Be specific.

3. Describe the three men who come to Charles's funeral. That is, give their physical characteristics and any peculiar details you noticed about each one.

   (a)

   (b)

   (c)

4. Mr. Bartholomew tells Regina about the relationship of the three rough men to her husband. What is the story?

5. (a) Does Cary Grant's character seem more or less guilty, judging by his behavior around Reggie?
   (b) Why do we—or do we not—suspect him? What specific incidents convinced you of his guilt—or innocence?

6. Slowly, one by one, the former OSS members are killed off. In what order?

   (a) Charles Lampert (Vass)
   (b)
   (c)
   (d)
   (e)

7. Everyone is looking for the $250,000 that Charles stole. Where is it?

8. What is the clue among Charles's belongings that finally alerts everyone to the location of the money?

9. The character played by Cary Grant has many aliases [other names]. List them:

   (a)
   (b)
   (c)
   (d)

10. Whom did you suspect was the killer among all these thieves? Did you change your mind more than once? Explain.

D.O.A. Quiz

1. Explain the movie title. What do the letters mean and why are they important to the story line of this film?

2. Sydney willingly comes along with Dex at first when he decides to investigate who poisoned him. True or false? Explain your answer.

3. Why does the widow Fitzwaring really object to Cookie and Nick's being together?

4. Who kills Cookie? Explain how it happens.

5. Why is the main theme of this film a kind of parody?

6. Was Bernard really the person who tried to kill Dex and Sydney with the nail gun? If not, who was it?

7. Who poisons Dex? How many others does this person kill and why?

8. How does the murderer get the poison?

9. When you were watching the film, who did you think poisoned Dex? How many times did you change your mind?

10. List the names, in order, of all the people who die while Dex is searching for his own murderer.

Traces of Red Quiz

1. What is the meaning of the film's title?

2. During the course of the film, how many different murder suspects are there? Describe the reasons why we suspect each one.

3. Why are the victims always women, and why are they women with whom Michael and Jack have both had sex?

4. Why does Ellen seduce Steve?

5. What are some of the red herrings in this plot?

6. How are women portrayed in this film?

7. What is the terrible injustice done to Gloria Wertz?

8. What characteristics of the suspense/thriller genre can be seen in this film?

9. What are some similarities between this film and *D.O.A.*?

10. What did you like best or least about this film?

Cape Fear Quiz

1. Why does Max Cady want revenge?

2. Why does Cady try to seduce Danny?

3. At what point does Cady become violent as well as manipulative?

4. Name three of the many things that Cady does to threaten Bowden and his family.

    (a)

    (b)

    (c)

5. Why does Lori Davis refuse to testify against Cady?

6. Why does Sam hire a private detective rather than let the police help him?

7. How does Cady know that the Bowden family has gone to Cape Fear?

8. Explain the twofold significance of the title.

    (a)
    (b)

9. Explain one of the themes of this movie. Give examples to support your answer.

10. Do you think Cady should have been jailed originally—fourteen years ago? Why or why not?